Launching the New Industrial Product

Philip Gisser

American Management Association

International standard book number: 0-8144-5275-2
Library of Congress catalog card number: 75-166555

FIRST PRINTING

Launching the New Industrial Product

Foreword

Book after book, article after article, tells us that new products are the lifeblood of industry. Reference after reference provides such quotes as: "Fifty percent of our company's business is based on products developed and marketed in the last ten years," "More than 72 percent of the nation's growth in sales volume comes from new products," "Most manufacturers cannot live without new products." Speech after speech and seminar after seminar covers in depth the development of new products, organizing for new-product development, minimizing new-product risk, and improving new-product payout. Some sources even tell us that new-product development is the single most important task of corporate management.

But most of this guidance material concentrates on the areas of development, market research, marketing testing, control procedures, technical optimization, and organization of a company for new-product leadership. Little has been published about the marketing of new products, and even less about the initial launching steps—the steps required to bring a new product to commercial status after the preliminary development activities have been completed and the decision made that the company has a viable product ready for marketing. What little has been written has largely covered new products in the consumer area; the industrial products area has been virtually ignored.

The purpose of this book is to cover the product-launching steps within the industrial sphere—to discuss, to probe, to analyze, and to recommend procedures that have been tested and successfully used in moving a new industrial product from the point where management says: "Yes, we have enough information to take the risk of commercial introduction. Yes, we are ready to go ahead and make this product commercial."

The steps involved in launching the new industrial product are largely communications-oriented. They involve communicating the information about the new product to potential customers. They involve handling and analyzing the communications from potential customers as they first become interested in the new product and later go through the evaluation steps that pave the way toward their using it within their own operations.

The use of these communications techniques involves understanding of a number of disciplines: sales training, advertising, public relations, technical writing, sales promotion, audiovisual presentation, inquiry handling and sales administration, to name a few. None of these disciplines will be covered in detail in this book. Rather, they will be covered only to the extent necessary for the reader to understand how best to judge their value and to coordinate their use. If the reader feels a need for further knowledge of any of these communications techniques, he must look to other sources—to the books and articles that have been written on these subjects, and to the various consultants and experts and organizations that serve these fields.

Philip Gisser

Contents

1

New Product Considerations

Approximately 30,000 new products are introduced within the American economy in a given year. One year later, 24,000 of them will no longer be on the market. This high mortality has been blamed time and again on lack of marketing research, on fundamental errors in estimating how great a need exists for the product at the price for which it is offered, on lack of technical expertise. And many times the blame has been put on failures in judging the capability of the company for producing the item in question.

These are unquestionably important factors in the failure of many new products, and increased sophistication in the launching steps will not decrease the number of failures resulting from them. But a large number of new products fail because of errors made during the launching stage. We do not know how many, because these failures are almost invariably attributed to other causes. But it is likely that hundreds of millions of dollars in development costs, and many times that amount in potential profits, are lost every year by American business because of the failure of products that would have succeeded had their initial market introduction been properly handled. And a comparable amount is lost in products, doomed to failure by other factors, that are carried too long after that failure should have been recognized. For it is one of the ironies of business that a well-handled product launching may accelerate the demise of a new product and thus be beneficial—otherwise, by lingering on the market, the product would consume unwarranted money and management energy.

DEFINING TERMS

If we are to truly probe the group of activities we call the new industrial product launch, we must first be sure that we use the same language. So let's take a little time to define the terms "new," "industrial," and "product."

Most important, perhaps, is the definition of "industrial" as it relates to a product. Most people agree generally but not precisely as to what constitutes an industrial product. Some define it simply as a product used in business and industry. But that definition leaves out a number of products that others would leave in—such as pharmaceuticals and farm implements. Perhaps the simplest, clearest definition of an industrial product, and in any case the one that will be used in this book is: "a material, item, or service that is purchased in the course of fulfilling a business goal (usually making money), by the purchaser or his employer." This distinguishes industrial products from consumer products that are bought for personal use. Thus, certain products, such as automobiles or even food, can be considered either industrial or consumer, depending on who is buying them and for what purpose. And indeed, the communications patterns and the motivational appeals will differ for the same product depending on whether the purchaser is buying it for personal consumption or as part of a business activity. This definition, then, emphasizes the buyer, more than the product. Though we talk of industrial and consumer "products," we are really forced to look at them in terms of markets.

Part of the problem in discussing new products is that everybody defines *new* in a different way. If the company that has been making machine screws starts selling wood screws, is that a new product? "Yes," says the seller. "No," says the buyer. If the company that has been making a 5 percent nickel steel begins to make a 6 percent nickel steel for sale to the same market, is that a new product? If the company that sells tape as an electrical insulating material starts promoting it as a method for binding wires to pipe, is that a new product? "Sometimes yes and sometimes no," say both seller and buyer. How then are we to define the simple word "new"?

The confusion that arises in defining new products has to do with two separate considerations. One is that "newness" is a matter of degree. The second is that as new products are normally defined, the newness can be in any of three dimensions: newness of the product to the market, newness of the product to the company, and newness of the market involved to the company. A product may be new, partly new, or old to the supplier independently of whether it is new, partly new, or old to the user. And it may be new, partly new, or old to the supplier independently of whether its market is new, partly new, or old to the supplier. Or it may be new or old to the user independently of whether the market is new or old to the supplier. Some examples, combined with Figure 1, should show these relationships.

Example 1

A nut and bolt manufacturer invents a totally new kind of fastener. This product is 100 percent new to the user, and 100

Figure 1. Degrees of newness of product.

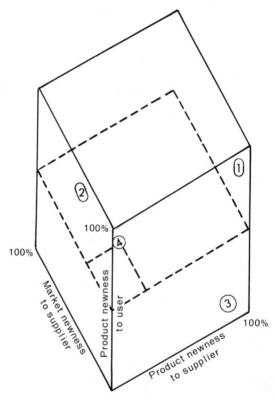

A new product can have any degree of newness in any of three dimensions — newness of the product to the user, newness of the product to the supplier, or newness of the market to the supplier.

percent new to the supplier, and the market is zero percent new to the supplier.

Example 2

A roller-bearing manufacturer decides to pursue sales opportunities in a segment of the market that had not previously used that type of bearing. This is 100 percent new to the user, zero percent new to the supplier, and a partly new (50 percent) market to the supplier.

Example 3

A manufacturer of fabricated stair rails for commercial buildings decides to add a line of aluminum windows for the same market. The product is zero percent new to the user, 100 percent new to the supplier, and the market is zero percent new to the supplier.

Example 4

A machine tool company refines its electronic control systems so thoroughly for its own use that it decides to market the control systems to all machine tool users and manufacturers. The product is partly new (50 percent) to the user, partly new (25 percent) to the supplier, and the market is partly new (35 percent) to the supplier.

As the examples show, "newness" and "oldness" are only the two extremes of the degree of differentiation. A product may be slightly related to that already produced by a company, it may be partially related, it may be almost completely different, or it may be totally different. And the same degrees of product newness can be applied from the point of view of the user, as can market newness vary from the point of view of the supplier.

Example 4, where each parameter of change is partial, is more the rule than the exception. And the degree of newness in each dimension becomes a major factor in determining the risks involved in a new product venture as well as the strategy and tactics needed to successfully introduce the new product.

The concept of a three-dimensional framework for defining "newness" of products explains why the introduction of a new product fits no standard mold. The position of the new product under consideration on this three-dimensional chart is one of the key factors in determining the strategy to be developed, the steps that must be taken, and the resources that must be applied for a successful introduction. With each new project somewhere in a scale of one to a hundred in each of three dimensions, the number of different situations can be extremely large. Small wonder that the lessons learned in one introduction are so seldom applicable to the next.

The word "product" implies something with physical form. Much of the industrial market today requires either "services" or mixed product and service systems. And these, from the viewpoint of both the buyer and seller, are no different from products in that they are needed to accomplish certain goals and that they cost money. The marketing of computer software or the providing of banking assistance, for example, are both so similar to the marketing of tangible products that we must consider them products of the company that supplies them. The phrase "products and services" will therefore be omitted in favor of including "service" as one particular type of "product," the term "product" referring to anything sold by one individual or organization to another.

SIGNIFICANCE OF THE LAUNCHING PROCESS

It is amazing how many new products are stunted forever by the failure of the introducing company to provide the funds necessary for an adequate launching. Obviously, in such cases, those who make the budgeting decision do not recognize the significance of the launching step to the profitability of the new product throughout its entire life cycle.

In a fairly common situation, a research department will have spent perhaps $100,000 in a given direction before it feels it has a chance to develop a particular technology into a profitable new product. And it may have spent $500,000 going down what proved to be blind alleys. Management may then authorize $300,000 more to make it possible for research to take the next logical step. The market research department invests $20,000 to $50,000 in a study and proposal so that the board of directors can then authorize additional research work and special facilities costing perhaps $1 million. They will later authorize perhaps $10 million in capital construction for production of the new product. When the product is ready to go, however, marketing will be given only three new salesmen, and advertising will be told to handle the introduction within its existing budget. A year later, when nothing much has happened with the new product and management is faced with appalling losses, one of two things may happen: either the product will be killed without marketing getting a fair chance to move the product off dead center, or marketing will be authorized to spend a massive amount. If the product is killed prematurely, the entire investment will have been wasted. If it is kept alive in the hopes that marketing can solve what turns out to be an unsolvable problem, then there is the likelihood of an additional six months to a year of extensive losses before the fact of a product failure is accepted.

The launching phase is one of the most critical in a new-product program, second only to those testing procedures that attempt to prove or disprove the new product's viability. To understand the significance of the launching phase, one need only put it into the context of the product life cycle, as shown in Figure 2. The basic shape of a product life cycle curve has been clearly outlined by Booz, Allen & Hamilton. It traces a product's path through the now familiar stages of introduction, growth, maturity, saturation, and decline. The time scale may vary from product to product, but the shape of the curve over whatever the product's lifespan may be is as true for any industrial product as it is for man.

If we concentrate on the profit curve rather than the sales curve, we see that during the introduction stage, profits are low or nonexistent. Somewhere during the growth phase, significant profits are normally shown; they are greatest in the latter stages. Decline of profits normally begins to take place at some point before the product reaches maturity.

Figure 2. The product life cycle.

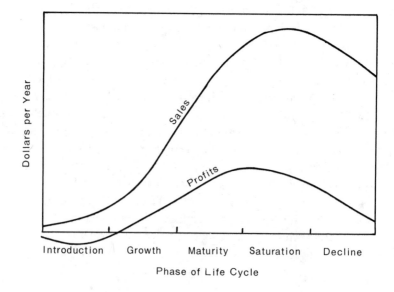

Phase of Life Cycle

The marketing pressures applied in the introduction phase have the effect of shifting the profit curve forward or backward in time. A soundly based and fully supported introduction will increase the original losses, but will reduce the time needed to achieve acceptance and to begin growth, thus shifting the curve to the left. A poorly planned and underfinanced introduction, while it decreases the losses at the early stage, shifts the growth phase far to the right on the time scale. Figure 3 shows that kind of effect.

Just as inevitable as the life cycle of the product, however, is the fact that for every successful new product there will someday be competition. And with the fast pace of technological advancement characteristic of the business world today, and the increasing pace that is projected for the future, the time lag before competition enters the field is constantly decreasing. As Figures 2 and 3 clearly show, the overall profits derived from a given product are largely generated during its growth and maturity phases.

The distribution of the potential market between a given company's product and competitive products during these highly profitable phases will depend very much on the degree to which the product had succeeded in penetrating its market before effective competition appeared. Three typical situations are diagramed in Figure 4. One shows a typical curve for a rapidly introduced product, one shows a typical curve for a normal introduction, and one shows a typical curve for a slow introduction.

The speed of the introduction, as noted before, shifts the curve to the right or left. For each of these curves the assumption is made that the curve begins to flatten shortly after effective competition is encountered in the field. The vertical line defines the point in time at which the competition becomes effective. In each case the product reaches its profitability peak after this time, but the level of profitability is vastly different for each of the situations. If the curves were redrawn to show cumulative profits the difference would be far more dramatic. The total return on a company's speculative investment in a new product might easily vary by a factor of 5 to 1 or 10 to 1 or 100 to 1 depending on the support given to the introductory program and how soon competition enters the field.

Figure 3.   Effect of introduction support (without competition).

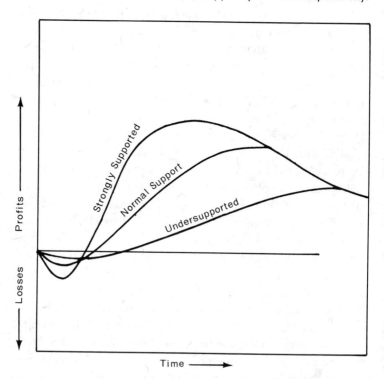

Even without the effect of competitive activity, a strongly supported new-product introduction provides a faster and larger return.

Figure 4. Effect of introduction support (with competition).

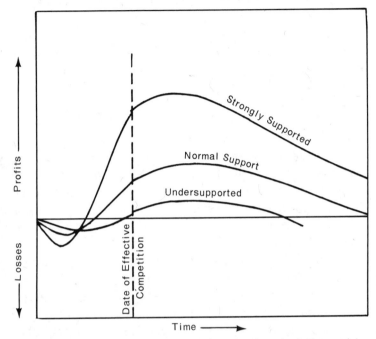

The long-range profitability of a product is strongly influenced by the degree of penetration achieved when effective competition enters the field.

TOWARD A RATIONAL FINANCIAL POLICY

It is obvious from the above analysis that from the point of view of new-product management, a heavier expenditure is called for in the pre-introduction and introduction stages than is needed after the product begins to gain momentum. But we must, of course, acknowledge that the better introductory program is almost without exception the more costly one, and the more costly one will naturally increase the losses expected during the early part of the product life cycle. The fact that in most cases the added costs are generally modest in relation to other elements of the new product investment, and minuscule in relation to the effect they may have on long-range cumulative profits, makes the investment no less costly—and no less speculative.

The point of view of the company's financial management may be very different from that of the product group. Profitability is normally looked at by financial people on an annual basis (with quarterly overtones), and a variety of other factors must be taken into account. Management must first of all balance the profit contributions of existing products with the profit drain of the new ones. And it must try to see that the stockholders balance their desire for immediate dividends with patience in awaiting what may be the long-deferred fruits of the new endeavor.

It is precisely the conflict between these points of view that gives the successful "young upstart" companies their initial bursts of growth. Operating on investment capital alone, these companies tend to give the new product the initial push it needs in money, in manpower, and in management attention. The more established companies, on the other hand, tend to limit their initial spending to a level that will not seriously reduce the company's overall profitability. Thus the small companies pull ahead rapidly until, their new products long since established, they, too, fall into the same profit trap when introducing subsequent new products.

There is a simple answer that satisfies the needs of both the current-profit-oriented financial manager and the sales-oriented marketing manager. It is simply to invest in the new product at the rate demanded by the product—with the heaviest expenditure at the front end, and the expenditure decreasing with time. But at the same time, the introduction costs will be amortized over a period ranging from three to five years.

Many companies amortize the development costs related to new products, and all companies amortize the capital equipment costs. Many companies are already grouping a variety of pre-start-up expenses and amortizing them. Relatively few, though, are taking advantage of the opportunity to include their initial market research, test marketing, sales training, advertising and publicity expenditures relating to the new product launching within the same category. If one looks at the introduction costs as an investment in the product's future, rather than as an expense against current and generally small sales, then he would have to say that an accounting procedure that defines such an investment as an expense distorts the picture.

Amortizing the introduction expenses permits investing in the new product with the heavy front-end investment normally demanded of good marketing judgment, while the financial reports show it as a gradually increasing expense as demanded by good financial judgment. Of course, if the new product effort turns out to be unsuccessful, a possibility for every new product, the company has to face the possibility of later write-offs. If this happens, though, the introduction expenses will probably be only a small portion of the total amount that will have to be written off.

THE EFFECTS OF ORGANIZATIONAL STRUCTURE

Most companies are organized so as to efficiently produce an existing product line and market it to an existing group of markets. This organization normally involves a complex structure of line and staff relationships, the details of which vary from company to company even within the same field. Each department in a particular company has its own goals, its own priorities, its own personality, and its own formal and informal relationships and communications patterns with other company departments. When we interject a new product or new market challenge into this organizational structure, a number of things happen. The nature of the new product or its markets often calls for new patterns of operation. And because the new product can expect a more rapid growth in the early phases of its development than can the existing products, it will require totally different means of communication and different priorities. The structure of a corporation, therefore, while ideal for existing products, can often be the largest single barrier to the development and introduction of a new product or the broadening of a product line to a new market area.

Let's look at a typical new product situation in an early stage. Its sales, of course, are small compared to those of the old product. Demand for research and development time, on the other hand, is tremendously greater for the new product. Thus the research and development department reorients its priorities and puts maximum emphasis on the new product, while production sees it at best as an annoyance and at worst as an obstacle to doing its basic job—that of getting out existing products. The salesmen, meanwhile, will have been helped to reach their utmost productivity by an incentive program based on their performance in selling existing products. So the new product, which will be low in volume during its earlier stages, is looked upon as a time-consumer that reduces their personal income. The traffic department tends to emphasize moving carload quantities instead of the small packages and special orders called for by the new-product-introduction pattern. And the credit department, which has adjusted its policies to deal with existing customers, will insist on applying those same policies to a new market area. Little can be done to see that these people adjust to the needs of new product marketing unless organizational patterns are changed.

The decision—a common one—to place a new product within an organization framework that was designed to move mature products is usually a decision to accept long delays in bringing the product to full commercialization. In a typical organization the departments involved in the introduction of a new product include:

1. General management
2. Market research
3. Research and development
4. Technical service
5. Production
6. Marketing
7. Advertising
8. Public relations
9. Traffic
10. Accounting
11. Credit
12. Personnel

The problem of welding these groups together in a way that will bring their efforts to maximum productivity for the new product, without destroying their effectiveness in producing and marketing mature existing products, is one of the most difficult problems that management faces. Yet if the fruits of new-product profits are to be theirs, it is a problem that must be solved.

The organizational options open to management are limited, though the variations within each option are many.

These options include

1. Fit the new product into the existing organization framework.

   Advantages: Minimum organizational disruption, minimum use of untested people.

   Disadvantages: Differences between departmental priorities destroy timetables. Inflexible policies by one or two departments can destroy effectiveness of introduction.

2. Give the responsibility to a committee representing the various departments involved.

   Advantages: Minimum organizational disruption. Little use of untried people. Some coordination achievable to help maintain priorities and timetables.

   Disadvantages: Demands of departmental priorities supersede those of the committee. Committee participation is generally considered a part-time activity secondary to the major needs of the department.

3. Form a task force representing the various departments and give responsibility for implementation to a full-time staff.

   Advantages: Under prodding of full-time staff, task force members give new-product needs higher priority within their departmental frameworks. Participation of various departments helps avoid misjudgments.

   Disadvantages: Higher priority to the company's task force may affect existing products. Staff requirements demand use of additional personnel, so untried personnel must fit somewhere within the structure, either on the task force or within the existing departments.

4. Set up a new unit whose sole objective is to bring the new product to commercialization.

   Advantages: Maximum effort will be concentrated by people involved. Tight coordination is achievable.

   Disadvantages: Large overhead incurred at the outset. Time is lost in establishing organizational structure. New and untested people must be given responsibilities.

As the reader can see, significant advantages and disadvantages accompany each of these approaches. Not only is there no approach that fits every situation, but the approaches that promise the best results are fraught with the greatest dangers. Compromises should and must be made.

If the management of a corporation keeps in mind the fact that the speed at which the new product can be successfully introduced is fundamental to its long-term profitability, and that that speed is directly related to the organization that is established to nurture the new-product opportunities it has identified, it will give a great deal of time and thought to the basic problem of how to organize the introduction of new products. And it will tend to take a greater risk as well. Whatever organizational route it chooses, the key decision will be "Who will have responsibility?"

Whichever of the above options is selected, it is important that one man only be given responsibility for directing and coordinating the new-product effort. We all know that a project without a head is no project at all and that where responsibilities are split, no one has responsibility. Every rule of corporate organization says that if there is a clearly defined job to be done, there must be someone with the clear responsibility to get it done. But selecting such an individual is difficult, as is defining his relationship to the rest of the organization.

The key problem in finding the logical project manager is that people with new-product experience are scarce. And people who combine new-product-introduction experience with specific knowledge of the product or its market or both are almost impossible to locate. The average corporation has had infrequent experience in introducing a new product. When a new product is successful, the man who has spear-headed its development is often moved with the new product to become general manager, or at least marketing manager, of that particular area of the business. To have him start all over again on a new and untried product would seem to him a demotion. So he cannot be considered for the position. The project manager of an unsuccessful venture, however, is likely to be available—if he is still employed by the company.

It is ironic that in the typical corporation, the only people within the organization who might be given responsibility for the new product are those who have never had such responsibility before or those who have, but have failed. Thus management is almost invariably faced with a choice between an unseasoned man or an unsuccessful one. Neither situation is likely to foster a feeling of security in the minds of the management group, which has so much to gain and lose from the effort.

Several approaches can be used to improve the chances of success. The most obvious one, of course, is to choose a seasoned executive with a record of success in the new-product-introduction area, take him away from his high-level job on a "leave of absence" basis, and give him responsibility for getting the project going. If he is backed up by a promising second-in-command, the No. 2 man will gain some experience in time for the next product introduction. This technique has the advantage that the executive so selected will have the respect of the other departments whose cooperation is so necessary for the success of the new venture.

Another approach is to assign responsibility to a bright, young, unseasoned individual. If this course is taken, however, it is wise to balance the risk involved by doing two things. One is to have him report at a level where the prestige of his superior can be used in places where his own is too weak to accomplish what has to be done. The second is to make available to him the services of an outside consultant who has the experience that he lacks.

Another alternative that should always be considered is to put the responsibility in the hands of someone with experience in a past product introduction that proved unsuccessful. If this is to be done, however, management should be quite certain that the cause for the product failure lay outside the control of the individual involved. In any case, management should be prepared to spend more time on the new product introduction with this type of selection.

If the reader is looking for recommendations rather than discussion, let him not go away unsatisfied. No system is best for all cases, but for most situations where new-product introduction is a relatively new experience to the company, a task force should be formed consisting of representatives of all the departments in question. These representatives should be instructed to devote a certain percentage of their time to the new-product introduction and to adjust the manpower needs of their departments accordingly. Accounting practices should be such that the time each man spends on the program is charged to the program.

As was emphasized previously, one man should be given full-time responsibility for directing the project, and he should be given the authority to demand performance by all the other departments involved. He should be able to call upon a top executive of the company and have that executive back him up in this demand. And whether or not this new-product "czar" has experience, it is desirable to obtain the services of a consultant experienced in a broad range of new-product–new-market introductions.

THE UNSUCCESSFUL PRODUCT

Strategists in the field of new business tell us that 80 percent of new products fail, and the reasons they ascribe include inadequate market intelligence, product deficiencies, higher costs than anticipated, poor timing, and competition. No one seems to have included "failure to provide adequately for the launching," although it is undoubtedly a factor in many of the reasons given above. It would be foolish to suggest that an adequately financed and well-planned launch will make a success of a product doomed to failure. If the product fails because it does not truly meet the needs of the market or because its price is too high or because its production idiosyncracies can never be mastered, a thoroughly planned and well-executed new product launch cannot be expected to save it. But in such a case, is a heavily front-ended program a wasted investment? The answer is usually no.

When a product is failing to progress at its expected rate, it usually isn't clear what the problem is. This is the usual time for a series of meetings between people having a variety of ideas, each of whom blames the lack of progress on a different element. Too often the problem will be diagnosed as a failure to provide sufficient marketing and communications effort, when in reality it is a failure to meet the needs of the marketplace. The net result is that a massive advertising and promotional program is launched six months or perhaps two years too late. And it, too, fails to make the product a success.

The cost of such a delay is usually much greater than the costs of any conceivable front-end promotional program. Even a crash promotional program normally represents only a fraction of the cost of continuing research, plant operations, technical services, sales staffing, and the diversion of management's time and energy in trying to solve the problem. If the launching is financed adequately in the first place and the product still fails to move, no one will try to argue to the effect that "the product is right, but it has been inadequately promoted." The variable of inadequate promotion is removed from consideration and the blame can much more easily be placed where it belongs.

If the deliberations at this point result in the product's being abandoned, so much the better. At least the product will have been abandoned at a much earlier stage, and this will usually mean a "savings" in the resources that otherwise would have been dissipated over what would have been a much longer period of time.

If this seems to be a one-sided recommendation for strong, heavily financed new-product introductions, it is. Just as an assault team must be given the resources that will enable it to establish a beachhead, so must a new product be supported adequately in its entrance into the marketplace. Anything less will doom the operation to failure, and the entire investment will be lost. If an error is to be made, let it be made on the side of supplying more, not less, than is needed.

The determination of how much capital is needed is the role of the strategist, and that subject will be discussed in later chapters. In any case, when the decision is made to put adequate resources behind the launch, care must be taken that other decisions are also properly made and carried out. If the launching is premature and the product has to go back to the laboratory for further work, a heavy communications sendoff can be more of an embarrassment than an asset. And if production capacity is not ready to handle the demand created by communications, the door will be left open to an earlier entrance by competition.

The properly managed, adequately funded product launch is not recommended as an element separate from other elements of a new-product program. It is only when the entire new-product program is properly handled that the launching step can fulfill the important role with which it is entrusted.

2

Information Needs for Strategy Development

The strategy for introducing a new product is, as has been mentioned, analogous to the strategy of a military group in establishing a beachhead. Will the company sneak up on competition with the new product or make a frontal assault? Will it begin on a wide front or concentrate its strength against a single area of the market? Will it use its heavy weapons to subdue the competition, or use psychological warfare to frighten it away? These basic options, as well as a variety of lesser ones, must all be considered.

The launching strategy for one new product may be completely different from that used for another. Why? The reasons lie in the wide number of factors that guide the decision maker in determining the optimum strategy. Ten people gathered around a conference table discussing the introduction plans for the first time will normally have ten different preferences as to strategy. But the more the ten people operate from the same information sources the more likely they will be to agree on the optimum introduction strategy. To narrow the choices down to the one or two most likely to be successful, certain basic information must be gathered. The information needs generally fall into the following classifications:

1. Product factors
2. Competitive factors
3. Market factors
4. Distribution factors
5. Resource factors
6. External factors

The kinds of information needed in each of these areas will be discussed in the following pages, as will the significance of the information to the later strategy development. Later sections detailing strategic approaches will pinpoint the utility of information and the potential dangers involved in each missing segment of information.

Even though time and money will limit the amount of information to be gathered, it makes sense to pursue each information path to at least a small degree rather than to omit any direction completely in favor of greater depth in the others. By pursuing each path at least briefly, the project manager will be more likely to be able to determine just how far he need probe each information area in order to feel comfortable with the information in hand. Part of the art of new-product introduction is being able to judge when enough information has been gathered in an area for it to be a realistic part of the strategy equation.

PRODUCT FACTORS

A great deal of information about the product itself must be known and understood before optimum market-entry approaches can be developed. The most important information includes the nature of the new product, its physical characteristics, degree of newness, advantages, disadvantages, price range, service requirements, and packaging. Normally this is the easiest type of information to obtain.

Nature of Product

The most obvious piece of information needed is, of course, the basic nature of the product. Are we talking about an engineered product designed for a specific application? Or is it a material? A service? A system? We have to find out the general nature of the thing we are talking about. Next we have to know its physical characteristics. How big is it? How much does it weigh? If it is a material, is it a liquid, a solid, or a gas? What nature of liquid, solid, or gas? Is it corrosive? Is it dangerous to handle? Considerations such as ease of handling and toxicity are important in determining sampling policies.

This basic kind of information is needed at two levels. The first level is the basic broad-scale information about the product characteristics needed to provide general guidance in developing the strategy used for introducing the product. For example, if we know that the product is a ten-ton machine, introduction strategy will call for bringing people to the machine rather than the other way around. The second level of information needed arises as we get close to product introduction. Then detailed specifications must be spelled out. We have to know exactly how high the product is, how wide, how long, how much it weighs, what its power requirements may be, and what its utility requirements are. For if we are going to bring people to the machine, we must arrange the time, the place, and the facilities.

Degree of Newness

One of the areas where people are most likely to mislead themselves is in the degree of newness of a new product. It may be both simpler and more pleasant to call new products and new services and new markets "new," but rarely are they absolutely new and different. Usually they are related to something already on the market, and it is the degree of that relationship or the degree of newness that has the most profound influence on market-entry strategy.

The degree of newness has two dimensions: degree of newness to the seller, degree of newness to the buyer. And the two bear little similarity to each other. If a company with no experience in the area starts to make fractional horsepower motors, those motors are a completely new product for that company. If a company that has been making large motors starts making fractional horsepower motors, the latter are partially new for that company. Yet in neither case would the motors be a new product from the point of view of the buyer. Similarly, when manufacturers of control equipment started switching from pneumatic control systems to electronic controls, they were making related new products. These were old products to the user in the sense that existing products did the same thing, but they were new in that they used a different technology with inherent advantages for certain situations where that technology could best be applied.

It is hard to find an example of a product that is totally new from the point of view of the user. The computer might fit this description, although in its initial applications, it did little that hadn't been done before—it merely did it faster and more economically. Yet we could probably score the computer at a 90 percent newness level from the point of view of the user in its initial introduction. And, similarly, the light bulb, which replaced the candle, cannot be classed as a 100 percent new product from the point of view of the marketplace.

The higher a product registers on the scale of "newness to market" the more complex introductory strategy must be. Often the concept must be explained, not merely the properties of a specific product. As a result, the communications costs will be higher, and this must be taken into account in the introduction strategy.

As an example, consider the introduction of a new computer terminal. If it is designed to replace a typical typewriter terminal, with a few new features giving it perhaps a 10 percent newness rating in the marketplace, its introduction strategy will not be complicated. The price must be equal to or lower than the price of comparable equipment. Communications must concentrate on the basic specifications and the few new features. The market is clearly defined as existing and potential time-sharing users.

But introduce a new type of terminal, which provides graphics capability, automatic hard copy, and a degree of computation capability, raising its degree of newness in the market to some 50 percent to 60 percent, and the options become far broader. Potential users cannot be defined since there are none at present. Pricing policies and other decisions also provide a wide range of choices. Communications has to concentrate on the concept and reach a broad audience. Software support, to facilitate conversion to graphics for the user, becomes an important element in marketing strategy. In short, the greater degree of newness to the market makes the introduction strategy far more complicated, far more expensive, and far more uncertain.

It is generally true that moving upward on the scale of newness to the market represents a mixed blessing. While opportunities are vastly increased, so too is the complexity of the introduction and the danger of falling into one or more traps.

Moving upward on the scale of newness to the company similarly presents both problems and opportunities. Obviously, it broadens the scope of the company and opens up new areas in which it can operate and in which it can expand in the future. But just as obviously, it means the company is entering new and uncharted waters where it can easily run aground. Production problems that never would arise where a familiar product was involved can plague an unfamiliar one. Cost estimates can go wrong by factors of 100 percent—or even 1,000 percent.

But even more dangerous are the marketing problems that arise. The company entering new areas can be hurt badly by things it doesn't know: that price lists may be meaningless in the market area, that new technologies may be on the verge of eliminating the product application, that union resistance may be a serious problem, that purchasers may have been burned in the past by an offering that sounded the same, or that reciprocity considerations can cut out half of the potential market.

How can the aspiring company avoid these unknown dangers? There is no ready formula. But where a company introducing a product new to the user is unfamiliar with the market, it takes a great risk in trying to shortcut any of the information-gathering steps outlined here. A company familiar with the market, on the other hand, may well be able to take such shortcuts.

Advantages and Disadvantages

The advantages and disadvantages of the new product represent information that is at the heart of an introduction strategy. This sounds like easy information to get, perhaps too fundamental a matter to dwell on at any length. But the project manager must be wary of his sources. Too often his only real source is the developers of the product. These are usually the technical or engineering people, who have been immersed in the project for so long a time that they are often less than objective in their evaluation. When they speak of product advantages, they often refer to "potential" advantages—advantages that can be realized only with further development.

Often, developing such advantages raises the cost beyond what is acceptable to the market. Often, too, the advantage cited is very real—but not terribly important. A fundamental new technique for machining metal may provide the capability of drilling oval holes—but unless a large segment of the market has a need for oval holes, other factors will far more significantly affect market acceptance.

Yet the error most often made in the process of looking at advantages is the overlooking or discounting of certain disadvantages. Learning about these is just as important as learning about product advantages, but it is considerably harder to do. People who have been intimately associated with the development of the product tend to blind themselves to its disadvantages. Yet almost every new product that changes a way of doing something will have both disadvantages and advantages. The new-product manager should play devil's advocate and truly evaluate all the negative aspects of the new product—before he learns about them from his potential customers.

In a large company structure, not all of the people who supposedly know about the product are describing the same product at the same stage of development. It is all too common to hear about the low cost of the product from one source and its wonderful properties from another, only to find out too late that the part of the line that is low-priced does not have all the wonderful properties, and conversely, that the part of the line with the wonderful properties is too costly to be competitive.

The project manager must also see to it that research and development programs test the product under use conditions, and that the negative reports are looked at critically and not simply explained away, as they so often are. He must satisfy himself that he has an objective view of both the advantages and the disadvantages, and that the former outweigh the latter, before he allows the project to be released to the marketplace.

Often, when people start describing the advantages it is difficult to know whether they are talking about the advantage of the particular product in competition with others in the same class, or the advantage of that particular class over alternative techniques of accomplishing the same thing. Product development people have a penchant for discussing generic advantages as though they were interchangeable with product advantages—a confusion that frequently is not clarified even in the final communications program.

The product manager for a new producer of titanium oxide pigment for paint is likely to hear internally (and perhaps repeat externally) that this pigment eliminates the danger of lead poisoning. This is true of all titanium oxide pigments when compared to lead pigments, but it is a meaningless claim in terms of other titanium oxide pigments. Pharmaceutical products, too, seem to frequently be involved in this confusion of generic with specific advantages. The antibiotic that by test does a better job of eliminating a specific bacterium than differently structured antibiotics may do no better a job than others of the same chemical structure sold under different trade names.

If such information is to be used, therefore, it is important that the project manager obtain a crystal-clear picture. One of the best ways to do so is the classic technique of writing down the advantages and disadvantages in a series of parallel columns, one for each directly competitive product within its generic class. A separate table of advantages and disadvantages should be made for that generic class as compared to all other possibilities the potential user has available to him to accomplish the same result.

Another area that should be looked at when probing the advantages is their tangibility. How clearly can they be demonstrated, how real, how apparent are they? A new finishing tool may provide a smoother surface—but how much smoother? Is it noticeable or does it have to be measured by a complex device? A new paint may afford greater protection than its competitors, but if it looks the same, this advantage may be hard to prove. A new product-entry strategy may well revolve around the techniques used to demonstrate an advantage that the product has but that is not very apparent.

We must all be alert to the fact that despite the very sophisticated tools at our disposal people tend to react first and to give the greatest weight to what they can evaluate with their own senses. A rough dull-finish paint may protect an industrial product better than would a good-looking glossy paint, but it will take a far greater communications effort to convince people of it. This author has seen a plastic cable compound with definite property advantages fail to penetrate its market simply because the surface finish did not look good—and even though it was destined for underground service. Of course, the tangibility of the advantages depends very largely on the knowledge level of the potential buyers. If you talk strength/weight ratio to a structural engineer, you may well persuade him to substitute aluminum or titanium for stainless steel. But try to sell on the same basis to an untrained house builder and it is almost impossible to do so.

Frequently a product's basic advantage lies in the statistical probability area—average deviation from tolerance, statistical probability of failure, probability of certain kinds of failures, and so on. All kinds of statisticians within your company will attest to the advantages. But unfortunately, there are usually very few people with statistical knowledge on the buyer's side. As a result, these kinds of advantages, though very, very real and very provable, are often the most difficult to communicate. Paradoxically, if you have a new product with a very important though highly intangible advantage and a relatively unimportant though tangible advantage, you may be able to do better in the marketplace by concentrating on the tangible advantage. But the decision has to be made in concert with many others. In any case, it is crucial to determine the advantages and the disadvantages objectively and then to assign weights on the basis of tangibility. This kind of objectivity should go a long way toward helping to define the optimum introduction strategy.

When given the specifications, the project manager in his role of devil's advocate should sharply question to what degree the forthcoming product will meet these specifications. When given performance data, he should probe the conditions under which the data was developed and question whether it is truly applicable to performance under real-life application conditions.

Many a product that has performed beautifully under

simulated conditions has proved too sensitive to environmental changes to meet the requirements of the environment for which it was intended. If the project manager sees a mechanic standing over the prototype with a screwdriver every time he goes past the shop, he should recognize it as a warning sign. And if the product hasn't been tested under extremes of temperature, humidity, and electrical supply, not to mention dust and fumes and vibration and maintenance neglect, he had best be prepared for some later surprises.

The project manager should be alert to problems of sensitivity to the operating environment and to the performance of the product under less than ideal conditions. For many a product otherwise better than its competition has failed in the marketplace simply because of inflexibility. This is not to say that a product that must be used within tight operating limits is doomed to failure. But such a product would need an introduction strategy different from that used for a product that could fit into any going process.

One breadwrap material made slow progress in the field until the manufacturer took it upon himself to modify the temperature controls of breadwrapping equipment to the tighter limits of his material. And a perfectly good dollar-bill changer that was successfully market-tested in an airport had to go back to the drawing boards after dozens were installed in steamy laundromats. Obviously, an earlier awareness of these sensitivities could have greatly speeded market penetration.

A clear understanding of the balance between a new product's advantages and disadvantages is a key element in developing strategy. Consider, for example, the history of polyethylene resins, the tough flexible plastic used in squeeze bottles and plastic bags. There was a time when film made from polyethylene was extremely tough and quite cloudy.

New resins were developed that had high clarity, but the improved clarity meant significant sacrifices in toughness. This led to a strategy that concentrated the introduction of this new family of resins in the soft-goods packaging area, where toughness was less important than clarity. Had it been introduced across the entire market, which at that time was dominated by applications that required a high degree of toughness—potato bags were one—it would have become another market-failure statistic.

Price Range

It may be unusual to look at price range as a basic element in marketing strategy inasmuch as price setting is in itself a strategic decision. But the pricing order of magnitude is normally fixed quite early—on the lower end by manufacturing costs and on the higher end by competitive considerations. Thus the range within which the product will eventually be priced is normally established at an early date and can be considered an information input before strategy is developed.

The price range is one of the most important "properties" of any new product. Price will determine not only the new product's eventual degree of market penetration, but where it can be sold and where it cannot be. It will also determine whether or not the product will supplant existing products and materials. The price should therefore be looked at carefully in all its ramifications by anyone attempting to enter a new market.

Price itself has several dimensions—an absolute dimension and a number of relative ones. We must look at the price in relation to both the price of competing products and to the total cost to the buyer. Price must first of all be considered in absolute terms. Are we talking about ten-cent, one-dollar, hundred-dollar, thousand-dollar, or million-dollar units? For strategy will, for obvious reasons, depend largely on these absolute figures.

Price must then be looked at in relation to competitive products that do essentially the same thing. If your pricing is potentially lower, the strategy would seem to be obvious: Promote it on the basis of its lower price, and market penetration will be easy to achieve. But it is rarely as simple as all that. In looking at the price of competitive products, one must not look so much at their current selling price as at their basic cost price, for this puts a floor under the retaliatory pricing possibilities of the competition. If your new product can be manufactured at a lower cost than can be achieved by the competitive products now on the market, then a price-dominated strategy is obviously sound. If the competitive products can be reduced in price to the same level or lower, however, little that is constructive can come of price-dominated strategy. Under such circumstances, your whole investment in market entry can be swept away by timely price retaliation on the part of those who already dominate the market. So price must be looked at first and foremost in relation to the *potential* price of the product it is designed to supplant.

Price must then be looked at in relation to other ways of doing things. Sometimes a new product will have a higher unit cost, but because of fundamental advantages, its use will result in a lower total cost on the part of the user. Where this is true, the cost will normally be different from user to user. In this situation, the strategy will be more complex, and the communications expenses that will be required to support the more complex strategy and the more complex message will be proportionately higher.

An example of some of these factors at work can be seen from the entry of high-density polyethylene plastic in competition with low-density polyethylene in the late 1950's. The high-density material was a stiff, almost rigid, material, in contrast to the softer, almost rubbery, low-density material, which had already established its place in the market. But the high-density material was also more expensive. It didn't take a sophisticated cost analysis to show that high-density material could be used in thinner sections to obtain approximately the same product properties as the lower-density material in thicker sections. Thus on a finished-unit to finished-unit comparison, the raw material cost for high-density material was lower, even though on a pound-to-pound basis it was higher.

But look for a moment at the obstacles raised. The unit weight of an item was determined not only by the stiffness limitations, but by shape, so that the amount of savings that could be obtained by switching from a low-density to a high-density material varied from item to item and had to be re-evaluated for each. And often the product had to be redesigned for the new material. With or without redesign, the specter of tooling costs was raised. A new multicavity injection mold can cost over $100,000. To modify an existing mold to handle a thinner section might involve a $10,000 to $20,000 expenditure. This cost had to be balanced against the savings in raw material. Another factor was that low-density polyethylene at that time had a considerable profit margin that permitted price reductions, and these did indeed take place.

The fact was that high-density polyethylene did supplant the low-density material in a number of its injection-molding applications, but after a much longer period of time than its original promoters had expected. It did, however, move much more rapidly into the blow-molding areas, where only an outer mold shape was required so that tooling changes became minimal. Whether the market-development strategy of the original producers of high-density polyethylene included aiming it toward blow-molding applications, where tooling costs would not become a factor, is not completely clear. But that is where the major penetrations were made, and in retrospect that is where the market-entry strategy should have been concentrated.

The example above is one of the simplest in the catalog of price/performance possibilities. Often new products involve totally new ways of doing things, which can involve massive capital investment and basic restructuring of the purchaser's organization in order to take full advantage of the benefits. The icebreaker that can carry oil from Alaska to the East Coast had to be evaluated against lower-cost conventional ships that traveled a longer route. A computer installation can provide tremendous savings to management, but only if whole departments are eliminated, others created, and new paper-work systems established.

It is obvious that the more complex the change that is required to take advantage of the economics of a new product, and the more capital investment that is needed, the more difficult will be the sale. And the market-entry strategy must be concentrated in those areas where the advantages are the greatest, or the dislocations the least, or both.

Another important way to look at price is in terms of the importance of the purchase to the user. When analyzed properly, this aspect often provides great insight as to the level at which the sales message must be directed. It is obvious that if you are introducing a new and improved paper clip you don't need to get the message across to upper-level executives. It is equally obvious that where you have a new and improved fuel for power stations, where the fuel represents a major portion of the cost of doing business, your message must be directed not only to the top purchasing people but perhaps to the presidents of the power companies as well. Similarly, the purchase of a new and improved $5,000 drill press will represent one kind of buying influence, the purchase of a multimillion-dollar rolling mill, another.

This factor bears less relation to the product being sold than to the nature of the company expected to buy the product. The purchasing influence for sulphuric acid at a steel plant where it is used in an auxiliary pickling operation is at a considerably lower level than the purchase of the same sulphuric acid for a fertilizer plant where it is a fundamental ingredient and represents a major segment of the cost.

Along with price considerations comes another consideration in mechanical goods—that of pricing options. The decision as to *what* price the company needs for the new product, including its options, may be essentially out of the hands of the marketing people, but the decision as to *how* to price may definitely be within. Should a product be priced at a top level with discounts allowed for options not accepted, or should it be priced at the lowest level, with premiums added for these? These questions depend completely on the competitive environment, and competitive practices in this respect should be looked at carefully, not so much as guidelines to be followed, but as practices to which creative alternatives can be developed—where options and approaches not yet undertaken by the competition can be utilized.

Service Requirements

It is obvious that the service required by a product is a key factor in establishing market introduction strategy. It is also obvious that assembled mechanical and electronic products need service. If they are unsophisticated mechanically, they can be satisfactorily serviced locally by established service organizations, and therefore little attention need be paid to this factor. But highly sophisticated products may require deployment of a separate service force, and the availability of such a force may be crucial in obtaining market acceptance. Materials and supplies also need service, though here the key contribution of the service staff is to help the potential user adapt his production system to the new product.

The significance of service is directly related to the importance of the product to the user. A key question is whether the product will be in the heart of the user's operations or peripheral. A product in peripheral use can normally be out of service for a few days; one in the heart of the operations cannot. For example, consider the dairy industry. If a packaging line breaks down because of the failure of a piece of equipment, the dairy is virtually out of business for the day. Introduction strategy might call for providing guaranteed one- or two-hour service, or it might call for paralleling parts of the system. Unfortunately, both of these alternatives are expensive—perhaps prohibitively so. If you can anticipate prohibitive expenses, though, the answer might be to avoid entering the market at all—or to limit area distribution to places where costs will not be prohibitive.

On the other hand, if the product you have sold the dairy is the conveyor belt that takes the finished containers out to the loading platform, or loads the trucks, the dairy operator can find an alternative means of accomplishing this should the equipment fail. There is therefore no need either to provide instant service or to promote the availability of that service as a market-introduction strategy.

Packaging

In looking at the nature of the product, we must bear in mind that its physical characteristics become intertwined with those of the package. While little can be done to change the physical characteristics of the product, innovative packaging can change the total effect of the product as perceived by the buyer. A dusty product, for example, can be shipped in a package that can be unloaded without dusting. This has the effect of changing the characteristics of the product—at least as viewed by the buyer. In looking at the strategy of introduction, one must therefore take into account not only the physical characteristics of the product, but any modifications of those characteristics that result from packaging.

COMPETITIVE FACTORS

One of the most obvious areas of information needs, and one frequently overlooked, is information on competitive products and competitor activities. Too often the "surprises" that hit a new product would not be surprises at all if a thorough study of the competition had been made before its introduction.

It is difficult to clearly separate the competitive factors that must be evaluated from the product factors discussed in the preceding pages. Though such areas as the nature of the product, physical characteristics, service requirements, and packaging can be looked at independently, such elements as advantages and disadvantages, degree of newness, and to some extent price range, are meaningful only when considered in relation to the competition. It is therefore obvious that a genuine study of product factors would include a study of all the products on the market that are either the same, or similar, or that can be used to accomplish the same end.

In the search for competitive information, it is important that we define competition in its broadest terms. We must include not only products similar to the contemplated entry, but every system that can, from the point of view of the potential buyer, do what he feels needs to be done. For example, a manufacturer preparing to introduce a new field-applied protective-coating material for underground pipe has to realize that other coating suppliers are not his only competition; he must also be aware of other ways of achieving pipeline protection. He must learn about the advantages, disadvantages, and costs of field pipe-wrapping systems, plant-applied plastic coatings, plastic sleeve systems, cathodic protection systems, and the use of noncorroding pipe materials as well. If he fails to look critically at these competitive elements, he may indeed satisfactorily introduce his new product, but he may be operating with a strategy likely to win for him a major share of a dying market.

While developing such information seems like a large order, it can be done if the will to do it exists. In most market areas, two or three major publications carry the bulk of the advertising, and one or two publications (not always the same ones) carry all the new-product releases. A study of these publications over a period of a year should identify most of the possible competitors and competitive systems.

It is usually worthwhile to formalize your study of the competition's communications. Space advertising, publicity articles, direct mail, literature, price lists, distributor promotion, and other sales promotion samples should be collected and evaluated, not only for the information they contain, but for a measure of the advertising expenditures of the competition. Literature and price lists on competitive products can usually be obtained by filling out the reader information cards that such publications include, or by writing directly to the company concerned. Obviously, some of these companies will not respond if it means they would be helping a competitor, but the literature can be easily obtained either through a customer who is working closely with you or through an outside consultant.

Beyond this, users of competitive products and competitive systems should be interviewed. This can provide not only a much clearer picture of problems to be faced than the published information, but also realistic information on any price deviations that may exist. Once obtained, the basic information about product differences can usually be put into a meaningful form with a simple chart, such as the one shown in Figure 5, listing the various competitive products on the horizontal scale and the various property characteristics or features on the vertical scale, with room to write in the significant information. While this sounds like a simple exercise, and indeed is, it is amazing how im-

Figure 5. A typical product-comparison chart.

Characteristics	New Product	Competition I	Competition II	Comments
Price	$815	$625/$1735 $695 (Digital)	$575/$620	
Voltage/ regulator	Built in	Needed	Built in	
Portable	Yes	No	No	
Records each test	No	No	No	
Solid-state circuits	Yes	No	No	Key to other advantages.
Zero drift	Almost none	Wide	Wide	Zero can be set once a day or less; others must be set each reading.
Memorizes zero setting	Yes	Yes	No	Once zero is set for each color, it holds for each color.
Repeatability	High	Low	Low	
Deviations between instruments	Low	High	High	Important when there are several instruments available.
Warmup time	Zero	One hour	One hour	Other units must remain on.
Time on	Small fraction	Continuous	Continuous	Leads to maintenance problems.
Polarizing filter	Built in	None	None	Permits reading wet or dry.
Maintenance frequency	Rare	Frequent	Frequent	
Speed	Frequently trade is left	Slow	Slow	Dealers arrange for repair services.
Ruggedness	Undergoes drop test	Separate probe subject to breakage		
Readout	Simple dial	Dial or digital	Complex dial	

portant this visual summary can become in identifying an optimum marketing strategy.

More important than the simple gathering of competitor information, however, is the evaluation of potential retaliatory tactics on the part of competition. It is axiomatic that the new product will be new only for a certain period of time. We must accept the fact that there will someday be competition and that the period of time in which a company has exclusivity will be growing shorter all the time.

With the sophisticated technological and marketing organizations operating around the world today, rarely is an area of potential development being studied by only one laboratory or a marketing opportunity being eyed by only one company. More likely, the company with a significant new product is only a short step ahead of two or three others whose work has been progressing just a little more slowly. When Du Pont, for example, introduced its fabulous new plastic product, nylon, it had it to itself for decades. By contrast, when it introduced polyacetal plastics early in the 1960s, it faced effective competition within six months.

We therefore have to assume that the period of exclusivity for the new product will be fairly short. But how short? If the time lag is sufficient to give you a good opportunity to establish a large market share for the new product, that is a welcome situation. But if a company with a dominant share of the market you plan to attack can provide a competitive product before you have yours really off the ground, it will probably benefit more from your promotional expenditures than will your company. It is important to look at the ability competitive companies have to make countermoves that would seriously hamper your penetration of the market. And your strategy should be built around the possibility of such retaliation.

Retaliation by competitors can take a variety of forms.

The most common, of course, is price reduction. If the key advantage of your new product is a lower price, a competitor can remove it as a threat by simply lowering his own price. Or if your product has some basic advantages, he may be able to lower his price to the point where he still has a price/performance advantage. It is therefore important that as you look at the existing price structure, you also measure the competitor's ability to reduce price.

His ability to do so will be based on his production cost. Though it will be difficult to get the information necessary to determine what that cost is, reasonable estimates can often be made by your production and engineering people simply by simulating the competitor's production technique. It is important in this type of analysis to look at incremental costs as well as fully accounted costs. The people now in the market have already made their plant investment, and they have to amortize its cost whether it operates or not. They can afford to retaliate by bringing their price down to the point where they would lose more by running than by shutting down. You, who have to justify an initial plant investment, can afford no such luxury.

As was pointed out above, it is important to evaluate the probability of concurrent development by other people—including those not now in the field as well as those already in it. This requires sophisticated knowledge of the technology, which can only be applied and analyzed by your technical or professional market-research people. It would be beyond the scope of this book to suggest how information such as this should be gained and how it should be evaluated, for it will differ from field to field and will differ greatly with the degree of technical sophistication involved. If the market research that usually precedes a new-product introduction does not make some assessment of the probability of others working concurrently on similar products, those in charge of the market research should go back and seek that as additional information.

Less difficult to evaluate but of equal importance is the reaction time of present competitors, that is, the time that the entrenched suppliers are likely to take to duplicate or supersede your market entry. Most companies dominant in their field have already developed more products than they have elected to commercialize. Frequently, they have within their research laboratories the technology to produce the new product that you are about to introduce, but it is usually not yet at the stage of development where it is ready for a full-scale commercial introduction or it would already have been introduced. Often such companies are very close to that point, however, and their reaction time then will be relatively fast. If so, your new product may become nothing more than a competitive product within a short time after introduction.

How quickly the competitive companies can react depends on a variety of factors: How important is the new product to them? How alert are they to the entering competition? How fast on their feet are these companies traditionally? How close are they to full commercialization? What effect will the commercialization of the new product have on the sales level of their existing products, and on the profitability of their total enterprise? All these considerations must be taken into account by your company in estimating the reaction time of the competition.

In considering possible retaliatory action, one should look at the possibility of established suppliers taking actions that might not make good business sense except for the effect that they would have on the company introducing the new product. An example might be a reduction in price below that which logic would dictate, or the announcement that a similar product will soon be available—whether or not development has begun. Such tactics are of questionable value and indeed of questionable legality, but the history of business abounds with them. Other, clearly legitimate, tactics are more commonly used, such as increasing the advertising expenditures, providing incentives for customers to sign long-term contracts, or making basic changes in sales, service, or credit policies.

It is often a worthwhile exercise for one or two people from the new-product-introduction team to do some role-playing—to put themselves in the shoes of a competitor to try to determine what would be the best course available to him. Whatever strategy your company develops for introducing the new product, it should keep all such retaliatory possibilities in mind.

MARKET FACTORS

Wherever a new product is directed toward a specific industrial market, it is essential that the product strategist know as much as possible about that market. The depth of information that might be needed is almost unlimited, so compromises in this area, more than any other, must almost always be made in determining the depth of investigation needed during the information-gathering phase. Where to make the compromise, though, is a key decision, one that may have a major effect on the outcome of the project.

The nature of the market into which the new product is introduced is fundamental to the selection of the entry strategy. The pharmaceutical market and the heavy equipment market will require completely different strategies. Similarly, market-introduction strategy for a new airplane would depend on whether the prime market involved the governmental, commercial, or civilian sector of the market. A thorough understanding of the marketplace for which the new product is intended is essential if one is to develop the kind of innovative strategy that will result in a satisfactory return for the dollar investment. Indeed the strategy may determine whether the new product lives or dies.

Foremost among the informational factors relating to the market is the potential sales volume. How much room is there for the product if the market were to accept the new product 100 percent? From this upper limit of potential sales a realistic evaluation must be made of the share of the market that the new product might expect to obtain. If it represents a technological breakthrough of major proportions, one can conceivably look to 100 percent of the market as the ultimate volume. More commonly, one should look for 2 percent or 5 percent or 10 percent of the market. While detailed analysis of the sales volume expected for the new product may well be needed for planning such things as production capacity, shipping, financing, manpower requirements, and so on, for purposes of developing market-entry strategy, only the order of magnitude is needed. For it is from this order of magnitude that one can develop reasonable expenditure-limitation figures.

If the potential volume is huge, the entry strategy can call for massive expenditures of money on the front end, with the objective of making the fastest possible penetration supportable by the other resources of the company. If the ultimate market is small, such expenditures cannot be justified, and dollar limitations on the entry cost may be the determining factor in strategy. For this reason it is important to measure the product's potential volume, and from that its potential profitability, so that the entry costs can be consistent with the ultimate profitability expected.

The second important market-evaluation factor involves defining potential buyers by industry and defining the people with purchasing influence within these industries by their job functions. Once developed, an estimate must be made of the total number of people who constitute the prime audience for the communications messages. A highly concentrated market such as steel or aluminum must be attacked in a very different way from a highly diversified market such as soft goods or retail establishments. Both the total resources needed and the distribution of budget between direct salesmen and mass communications will be strongly influenced by the number of potential buyers.

Information on the buying industries is usually easy to find by traditional market-research techniques. Where they are not clearly defined, introduction strategy may well call for mass-communications programs aimed at identifying markets beyond those presently being considered.

Identification of the people who are the buying influences within the target industries is often more difficult. A formal study of industry buying practices, or an informal survey of parallel products, can often go a long way toward answering the question. Where the information is not easily available, it can often be inferred from earlier derived data on the size of the expenditure relative to the size of the user's business.

In industries made up largely of small businesses, the buying influences are usually easier to define: the top man and his key assistant. For undifferentiated products that are of relatively minor importance to the buying company, the purchasing agent or buyer is the important man. But for differentiated products, the purchasing agent must be considered only one of a number of purchasing influences. For systems sales or for a product that requires a change in systems, the purchasing influences will include the various departments that will be involved in the system change. A computer system decision, for example, can easily involve accounting, traffic, warehousing, and marketing as well as systems management. And a new materials-handling system may well involve packaging changes, which in turn will call for production and sales involvement. Whoever the primary and secondary buying influences may turn out to be, and wherever they may fit into the corporate structure, it is of the utmost importance that we identify them. Without such identification, no efficient mass-communications program can be established, nor can sales operate with any degree of effectiveness.

It is not enough, though, to have information that merely identifies the buyer and the degree of influence he exerts. It is equally important to learn how the typical buyer thinks, with special emphasis on the obstacles that are likely to stand between him and a favorable purchase decision. Information on buyer attitudes is too often overlooked in the information-gathering process. A perfectly good product, for example, can easily fail if it has recently been preceded by a poor product that made similar claims—unless the introduction strategy takes this into account. Buyer attitudes can often be determined by survey techniques, and they will often lead to conclusions opposite to those that evolve from more traditional "buying practices" studies. For example, a "buying practice" study of an industry may show that leasing is the prevalent technique for marketing machinery, but an attitude study will show that the buyers dislike the leasing pattern and resent having been forced into it by suppliers who dominated the market from a technical standpoint.

It is important, too, to assess both the risks and the benefits to the buying company in making a positive purchasing decision, and to make the same assessment for each man in the buying decision chain. And along with this we must assess the ability of each man to evaluate the risks and benefits to which the buying decision exposes him. The risk/benefit ratio, we will see in a later chapter, is one of the more important considerations for strategy development, so the better the information on risks, benefits, and evaluation capability, the more likely the project manager will be to evolve a successful introduction strategy.

A primary area of information commonly needed is the degree and classification of industry segmentation. Each industry has its own classic pattern. Paint breaks down into "industrial finishes" and "trade sales." Computers are classified according to "mainframe," "peripherals," and "software." The electronic market is commonly segmented into "military," "aerospace," "communications," "home entertainment," and "control." Every industry is segmented by size: the top 3 or 10 or 30 companies that account for 70 percent or 80 percent or 90 percent of the business. Many industries are segmented by captive and independent operations—some captive to suppliers, others captive to customers.

Of equal importance to the strategist, though harder to identify, are some of the more informal segmentation patterns: the price leaders and price followers, the honest elements and the thieves, the well-capitalized and the undercapitalized, the innovators and the conservatives, the tightly organized and the freewheeling companies, the ones who use process A and the ones who use process B, the quality houses and the price-cutters.

It usually pays to study an industry in sufficient depth to identify the informal differentiation, for upon this knowledge many a successful new-product-introduction strategy has been built.

Another market factor that must be closely studied and

clearly understood before a realistic market-entry strategy can be developed is the business patterns within the market. These include the pricing, discount, and credit practices that prevail within the industry. Only by understanding these business patterns can we clearly see which are the elements we must conform to, and which are the elements that offer us the opportunity for innovation.

Even past practices on new-product introductions must be looked at. If new products have previously been introduced that have claimed to perform as yours is expected to perform, but have been unsuccessful, this will provide a major obstacle to overcome in your introductory strategy. And if the industry has been subjected to a series of speculative new-product introductions—introductions made before the product has been fully developed—your product-introduction strategy must have within it an element of "proof" that your product does indeed exist.

These examples may seem far-fetched but they do, nevertheless, exist. The computer-peripherals market has been one wherein companies have too frequently announced new products that have never seen the light of day. It may have been a successful strategy for the first few manufacturers who used announcements to test salability but the result of its overuse is that the market now questions all new-product announcements. A new market entry in the computer-peripherals field must take this into account or face some disappointments in its early market penetration.

Other acceptance patterns must be looked at closely, too. Some industries will jump at new innovations. Others are slow to respond. Some have a series of built-in evaluation steps, accepted as a standard within that market. If such is the case, then entry strategy must aim at reducing the time lag involved in these steps to a minimum.

Another important market factor to consider is promotional opportunities. They might involve a trade show, a technical society meeting, or some other significant communications vehicle specifically aimed at the market. The plastics industry, for example, has one major trade show every two-and-one-half years, the dairy industry one every four years. Depending on the nature of the product, this may affect the timing of the introduction and the manner in which the new product is introduced. For example, if the new product is a major piece of heavy equipment, and the timing is compatible, introductory strategy should probably be built around the demonstration of this unit at the show. If, on the other hand, it is something that need not be seen, and that would probably not tend to dominate the show, strategy would call for avoiding the show on the grounds that the message would probably be buried among the other new products introduced at the same time.

Another important market factor is the communications environment. The audience for your new-product message is not sitting out there waiting to hear about your great new contribution to their well-being. It is subjected to a large number of messages each day, many of them sounding surprisingly alike. If a company is going to be successful in introducing a new product, it is important that its voice be heard above the din. But how loud must it raise its voice to be heard? The answer varies with the product and it varies with the industry. It is extremely important to look carefully at all of the public utterances of the competition. How much are they advertising? Where? What are they saying? How much appears in editorial columns about them? What does the competition's literature look like? Or its direct mail? A study of the magazines in the industry will usually reveal the general pattern of competitive activity. A more thorough study, however, can determine such detail as how much the competition is spending on communications. Or advertising figures for certain product areas and companies are available in reports offered by private services.

Few factors have more influence on the dollar investment needed for a successful new-product introduction than the communications environment. The cost of being heard over the communications noise is roughly the same for both large-potential and small-potential products. It costs a certain amount to communicate to a market whether or not the profit potential of the product is sufficient to support that communications investment. Many a new product has failed because the maximum investment it could support was insufficient to penetrate the noise level and win a fair hearing. It is important to know how big the game we're planning to enter is at an early stage—before the market-entry strategy moves too far along.

The market-information needs for new-product launching are so many and so varied that even the outline above leaves many areas untouched. To formalize the procedure in every area would probably involve unreasonable time and unreasonable expense. Yet, for anyone but an industry expert, it is dangerous to rely on casual judgments.

It is obvious that the need for formal information-gathering in this area is far greater for a company entering a new market than for a company introducing a new product into a market it is already serving. The company with market familiarity has far more going for it and a far greater chance of success because of its better knowledge. The company entering a new market with a new or an old product must pay careful attention to its information needs, lest it make marketing errors of such a large scale that recovery is impossible.

For such a company, often the best way of developing this

information is to add someone to the staff who has had lengthy experience within the industry—someone who is intimately familiar with the key people, the reputations of the various companies, the business practices, and so on. Not only can he provide the needed information quickly and efficiently, but he may well know the many things that it seems unnecessary to know—until the product is well on its way into the market.

DISTRIBUTION FACTORS

The manner in which a product is distributed can often make the difference between success and failure in new-product introduction. Distribution policies may prove the new product's undoing, or they may provide the opportunity that enables it to step out ahead of its competitors. The first step in arriving at an optimum distribution policy is to gather information on competitors and to thoroughly evaluate their existing distribution practices. This means finding out answers to questions such as these: Do they use their own salesmen, or do they sell through distributors? Are distributor territories protected, semiprotected, or are they in competition with each other? What does the distributor contract look like? What is the commission basis? What is the pricing and discount practice concerning distributors? Do the companies "participate" in distributor price cutting? If direct selling is used, are salesmen salaried, or paid commission, or are they compensated by a combination of the two? What combination? There are a million and one questions to be asked.

Usually an industry will follow a particular pattern, or failing that, two patterns, one for the larger companies and another for the smaller. It is important to look at them and make your own judgment as to whether or not they are truly necessary for marketing and distributing that kind of product to that kind of market. Perhaps they have arisen from conditions that no longer prevail and are now based only on habit. If the former is the case the company had best follow established distribution lines, using the pattern for the industry as a guide. If the latter is the case, there may be a real opportunity for developing a new distribution pattern.

The question of distribution pattern is far more important for a company entering a new market than for one introducing a new product into familiar territory. The company operating in a familiar market will generally fit the distribution plan for the new product into its existing structure.

But for a company entering a new market the problem is far more complex. Even if logic tells you that a direct sales force is the proper answer to your distribution needs, to follow that course from the beginning creates a whole set of additional problems. The sales staff must be recruited and trained—a process that takes more time than most people realize. Sales offices must be established. A heavy fixed investment is incurred that might easily drain away the available resources if technical or production snags are encountered or if market acceptance is slower than expected.

Because of these problems the more common technique is to use existing manufacturers' representatives or distributor organizations—at least until the product is established to the point where it can support a direct selling force. Even here, time must be allowed for effective training of the representatives, though far less time than would be needed to build a separate force. And a greater reliance must be placed on the mass communications to carry the selling message past the sometimes unreliable middleman.

Distribution policy, of course, goes far beyond the selling

structure. Shipping, warehousing, and delivery service all fall into the same basic framework. Again, the best source of information is a close study of industry practices—both to establish your minimum criteria, and to identify opportunity. If competitors provide overnight deliveries from a dozen strategically located warehouses, you had best establish a comparable capability. If the best they provide is two-week service in some areas where you have warehousing activities for other products, you may have the key to your market-entry strategy.

For some products the major problem in the distribution area is the obsolete-inventory problem. If the new product is an improvement on an existing product that your company already makes, what is to be done about your inventory as well as the inventory in the hands of dealers? Will it be immediately made obsolete by the new product? If so, the question of what to do about it may loom large in the development of the new-product-introduction strategy.

RESOURCE FACTORS

A key area in the development of strategy for a new-product introduction is evaluation of the resources available to support it. Far more than any other considerations, limitations in available resources require market-entry strategies that vary considerably from "ideal" strategies. Four key resource areas must be considered—technical manpower availability, marketing manpower availability, production capability, and money availability.

It is obvious, of course, that the heavy expenditure of marketing dollars is not warranted if it will produce more sales than the production capabilities can support. Similarly a broad assault on the market might be warranted from every consideration—except that there aren't enough salesmen available to make such an assault. And if money is the limitation, as it often is, this is in itself sufficient reason to set a strategy that concentrates on one segment of the market instead of attempting to dissipate the available funds over a broad front.

Almost never are all these resources available in the amounts needed to provide an ideal new-product introduction. It is therefore important that the availability of each be assessed fully and objectively if the market-entry strategy is to be realistic. These resources can hardly be looked at independently. Money can replace any of the other three resources—but only if it is accompanied by time: A decision to provide additional technical manpower can take months or years to implement no matter how much money is behind it.

Little need be said about how to measure the marketing manpower or the technical manpower available. It should be evaluated within the company with full knowledge of the other demands that might be made on the same people. The length of time required to train additional people must be factored in, so that the potential availability can be determined along with the current availability.

Production capability for some products may also be highly limited. For others production may be easily expanded.

In all cases introduction strategy should call for expanding sales approximately at a pace geared to production capability. However, one word of caution here. Production capability can usually be quite accurately assessed. Market penetration at any given time is extremely difficult to assess. Too often a market introduction is stifled by an attitude that the product offers such great benefits that the market will rise to the offering and demand the new product at a pace far beyond the capability of the company to produce—a situation that rarely occurs in fact. In the new-product introductions in which this author has been involved, this fear was expressed over 75 percent of the time, usually by those involved in production. In actual fact, it occurred less than 5 percent of the time. And time was often lost gearing up the marketing and communications activities after the true situation had been realized.

The rate at which a new product penetrates the market is usually considerably slower than the rate originally anticipated. We must all face the fact that however much we may fear that marketing will outstrip production, it usually turns out the other way around. And if marketing does outpace production, it rarely causes serious difficulties. It does, in fact, create the kind of pressure that can result in receiving a better price for the new product.

The new-product manager would be well-advised to develop a strategy that keeps constant pressure on the production people. If his projections are correct and he is embarrassed about the consequences, he will find it far less embarrassing to himself, and less detrimental to the product's future, than an error in the other direction.

The availability of funds is, of course, another matter. It is an obvious and total limitation. Within any corporation there are many demands upon funds and it is management's responsibility to allocate them in such a way as to optimize its total return from all its investments. This allocation, then, is not always the amount that would optimize the return from a particular new-product investment.

In almost every new-product introduction in which this author has been involved someone has at one time said: "Let's develop a full program and see what it will cost to really do this introduction right." A lot of time and energy is spent in what turns out to be a futile exercise, because the amount needed to "do it right" is almost always greater than management is willing to allocate. The key question in strategy development is how to utilize the financial resources available to get the greatest return from the new product.

In many ways such planning is analogous to a military operation. Rarely does a general have the option of assembling as many forces as he needs to overwhelm his opponents. Usually he must decide how he can be most effective with the limited forces at hand.

While determining the maximum desirable is usually an unwarranted exercise, determining the minimum is quite important. If management is looking for guidance as to what the new-product-introduction costs should be, several possible strategies should be worked out, their costs estimated, and the rate of market penetration achievable should be estimated. This will give management the guidance it needs in its allocation decisions.

One accounting factor should be considered in determining the amount of money available for a new project. In a large company where management seeks to support the new-product introduction on a year-to-year basis from the profits of its other operations, external considerations may limit the financial resources for the new product severely. As mentioned, a simple change in accounting procedures may make sufficient funds available. The money spent in introducing the new product in its initial communications efforts is the kind of expense that has value throughout the life of the product. It is completely realistic and acceptable accounting practice to amortize the introduction expenses, including the advertising costs, over a period of at least three years. This simple change in accounting practices can often make the difference between a successful and an unsuccessful introduction.

EXTERNAL FACTORS

The last group of factors that must be looked at critically and objectively before a strategy is developed are the external ones—those relating to the things that are going on completely outside the control of the company and its industry. Many of these external factors can have profound effects on the success and growth of the new product. Government regulations, new and old, are typical external factors. So are social attitudes, public opinion, building codes, union practices, safety considerations, environmental control problems, and the state of the economy.

Most of these are too obvious in their effect, and too narrow in their relation to specific products, to warrant detailed discussion here. Obviously, a new product in the medical area must follow stringently the pattern for new-product introduction established by the Food & Drug Administration. The introduction of a product that requires major capital investment by the prospective buyers will be strongly influenced by prevailing interest rates, the availability of capital and the Internal Revenue Service's policy toward depreciation allowances. A new product entering the construction area must in its introduction strategy take into account not only the building codes that affect it, but also the differences between the building codes in the different areas in which it hopes to operate. It must also take into account union attitudes toward the new product. A product that saves a great deal of money at the expense of labor can run into severe problems because labor does not want to give up its "right" to do that particular kind of work.

Environmental control considerations are looming more and more important in the development of new products. If the product is packaged in a disposable container, or is itself disposable, serious thought must be given to how disposal will be handled. It is increasingly obvious that the day when this decision can be left to the buyer is past. Similarly, the new product whose use might result in some degree of air or water pollution must have the answers to these important questions before it will make any real penetration into its intended market.

The consumer protectionists must be anticipated as well. The manufacturer of a product that will end up in food, or cosmetics, or clothing, or in any other personal-contact item, must know beforehand and be able to establish that it will not cause any detrimental side effects.

The important thing about the external factors is that there is usually little that can be done about changing them. But in planning a new-product introduction one must look carefully at the world around us to see how it will affect the new products. And we must look beyond the current attitudes and regulations to see whether changes are forthcoming in these external factors. Once we have identified the external factors and their probable effects, the new product and its introduction strategy must be adapted to them—not the other way around.

I recall vividly the unsuccessful development of a plastic gasoline tank, which failed only because of changes in these external factors. While hundreds of thousands of dollars were being spent by several companies in the plastics industry to develop gas tanks that would match the properties of existing steel gasoline tanks, new regulations for automotive crash proofing and air-pollution control were being developed in response to government pressure and pressure brought by individuals concerned with safety and the environment. The net effect was that when the gas tank achieved the stage of development that was originally thought to be its goal, it could not meet the impact and emission standards being established for the future. It might have taken a farsighted prophet to have predicted the change in requirements, but such a prophet would have saved a number of companies a great deal of money.

3

Developing the Strategy

The preceding chapter was devoted to the information needed by the project manager before he can make the strategic decisions that can mean the difference between product success and product failure. It also discussed the significance of some of that information. Presumably, then, at some point in time (and it is rarely a single point), the project manager has a mass of vital information at his fingertips.

With this information, and with some feeling for the market, its structure, and the opportunities it offers, the project manager and his group face the most important part of their task—the development of an optimum strategy for the new-product introduction. Strategy is such a common term that we often use it without clearly understanding it. And like so many common terms, it seems to have different meanings for different people. Strategy, as we use it here, is the mix of policy decisions that serve as a framework for optimum introduction of new industrial products.

Strategy development in business, as mentioned before, is

similar to military strategy development. One looks at the enemy, at the terrain, at the resources at his command and then decides whether to attack across the whole front, to attack an area of enemy weakness, to feint in one direction while attacking in another, or to attempt an encirclement of the enemy's position. The policy decisions made on total forces committed, the position of the forces, mix of forces, the type of tactics that will be used, and criteria for judging activity, all come under the heading of strategy, while the action steps are considered tactics.

Similarly in marketing, the same commitment of resources, mix of type of resources, and allocation of resources, as well as tactical guidelines and criteria that must be met, all come under the category of strategy.

Tactics, on the other hand, relate to the actual activities of each of the segments of the introductory program. For example, the decision to utilize distributors in all but the three largest market areas while using company salesmen in those areas is a strategic decision. The selection of the particular distributors, however, is a tactical decision. Or again, the decision to invest a million dollars in promotion is strategic, but the distribution of the funds to various media is tactical. Just as in a military operation, however, the lines between strategy and tactics are not always clearly drawn. A decision to concentrate on direct mail for a product introduction is tactical in that it defines media, but strategic in that the media decision fixes the amount of promotional investment needed.

The development of a product-entry strategy involves the making of a number of key decisions. These include

1. Timing
2. Budget determination
3. Allocation of budget

4. Market positioning
5. Risk/benefit ratio determination
6. Pricing and terms
7. Distribution patterns
8. Service policies
9. Communications strategy

Each of these factors will be covered in detail in following sections.

TIMING THE LAUNCH

Normally a product is launched in several steps and over a period of time rather than as a single step at a single point in time. For example, if a company is introducing a new product related to one it already produces and that will be going to the same markets, it will probably want to call this to the attention of its current customers before it makes a public announcement. Indeed, it may also make good sense to call it to the attention of certain important buyers who are customers of competitors before making the announcement. A product that has a heavy service requirement, for which nation-wide service facilities are not available, can usually not be announced nationally. There must be a series of local announcements, and the introductory plan must call for time-tabling the introductions in each location. And there are times when a major industrial show is scheduled before a company is ready to make its public announcement. In such a situation, the company might take advantage of the presence of key potential buyers by showing the product behind the scenes at the show so that it can be demonstrated to selected people.

No matter what steps are called for, however, there is one point in the course of the new-product introduction where a clear-cut milestone is passed. That is the public introduction. Prior to this, one can look at the product as though it were in an experimental or developmental stage, available on a selective basis. After the announcement it is a full-fledged product, available to anyone. The public announcement may take place at a trade show, or at a meeting of potential customers, or through a broad announcement to the salesmen, or in the most common case, by a press release to trade publications.

Once this public announcement has been made, a number of things happen, both good and bad. The entire market finds out about the availability of the product. The company no longer has the option of selecting the most important people as its customers. The press is free to print anything it wants about the product, good or bad. Competition is quickly brought up to date on the product with far more reliable information than it had in the past. Competitive salesmen suddenly feel free to discuss your product's advantages, and more commonly, its disadvantages, with your potential customers. And your company at this time has something of an obligation to provide details to most of the people who ask about the product—details on performance, on specifications, on pricing. Any failure to provide such details will be considered evidence that the product is not quite as ready as your announcement indicates.

But there are as many, if not more, advantages to the public release. The trade press will now prove very helpful in conveying the information to your potential customers. It will do this not only in special articles devoted exclusively to the new product but in roundup features that cover the area your product serves.

Such publicity, combined with other mass communications techniques, can carry the product message far beyond your known potential customers. This author has seen more than one product that failed in the area for which it was intended, but that turned out to be a success because unanticipated applications were uncovered in others.

When the public announcement is made, other good things occur inside the company. The salesmen feel free to innovate, to carry the message to a wider prospect list, and to work on their own without relying on detailed supervision from the head office. And many decisions that have to be made before this public disclosure, such as establishing clear-cut price structure and credit policies, remove the detail load of one-at-a-time decisions from the project management group that burdened it during the development phase.

This point at which a new product achieves public status is very much like the point at which the butterfly emerges from its cocoon and starts to spread its wings. But there are problems associated with freedom, too. Once a product has gone public, it is difficult to change fundamental decisions already made. If you have underpriced the product it is extremely difficult to raise the price later. If the product develops technical bugs and must be withdrawn from the market until they are corrected, there is no hiding the fact from either customers or competitors.

In short, the new product that your company has been carefully developing and nurturing has now become public with all the advantages and disadvantages associated with life in a goldfish bowl. Let there be no mistake in judging the advantages, however. Where several companies are moving toward the same new-product area at the same time, the first one to publicly introduce the product will gain a tremendous advantage. His is the product that says "new," that significant word which, when properly backed up, can buy two or three or five dollars' worth of communications for every dollar spent by the competitors in saying "me too." The first to announce will be the center of attraction in press reports. The others will have to settle for one-paragraph announcements. Getting there first can mean the trade name that later becomes almost generic and makes the No. 2 competitor wring his hands when he sees his purchase orders with your trade name on them. In a competitive situation, and there are few situations that are not competitive, the first one into the market sets the pace and stands ready to dominate the market as long as he continues to exercise his leadership.

On the surface, the ideal time for public introduction of the new product seems a simple matter to decide. Simply wait until all the market-testing work is done, and then, when you are sure you have a good and reliable product, announce it publicly. But the real world of business seldom offers so simple a course. The point at which you are "sure" is a matter of opinion, not fact. And different people have different opinions as to when that point is reached. Usually the technical people want far more testing before they feel ready to say the product is ready to go to market. The marketing people, on the other hand, whose weather eye is more attuned to competitive activity, are usually too ready to jump the gun and release the product before it is completely ready.

Inevitably, compromises must be made. It is sad but true that you must usually introduce a new product before it is "absolutely sure." If you wait until you are "sure," you are almost certainly going to be No. 2 in the field rather than No. 1. And the cost of keeping a product in the costly developmental stage, rather than in the profit-producing stage, is not one that endears the project to upper management forever. The decision on the time for public introduction demands that a calculated risk be taken. The outcome of the decision will be the measure of the wisdom of the man who makes that timing decision.

The timing of the new-product introduction is such a critical decision, and one so subjective in its nature, that it is best left in the hands of an executive decision maker with a record of good judgment in similar areas. He must listen to the people involved. He must probe the attitudes of the technical people. He must probe the attitudes of the marketing people. He must probe deeply for the attitude of everyone involved. But in the end, he must make the decision—and once the product is public, he must live with that decision. He probably won't be exactly right, but he is usually better off in erring on the early side. To err on the late side usually costs far more in lost opportunity than is lost in the embarrassment of a slightly premature release.

DETERMINING THE BUDGET

One of the most difficult and most important strategic decisions of new-product introduction is determining the amount of the funds to be allocated to the project, or fixing the budget for the product-launching. A high initial investment can go a long way toward assuring product success. It can increase the rate of market penetration and therefore the ultimate profitability and return on investment of the entire project. On the other hand, if the product has some inherent unidentified problems that will delay or completely defeat the project, much of the value of this high investment will be lost.

Almost never is a decision made to back a new-product introduction with all the capital that it can utilize. Occasionally the decision is made to allocate something close to that amount. And at the other end of the scale, decisions are sometimes made to provide so little funding that the product's chances of success are seriously impaired. As a general rule, the decision is somewhere between these two extremes.

It is far more common for the product-launching to be underfunded than overfunded. This is so for a number of reasons. One, surprisingly, is the fact that launching costs seem so often to be a "surprise" to the product planners. In the consumer area, introduction costs and later advertising costs are so great that they must be considered from the inception of the project. Indeed, because of the significance of these costs, marketing-oriented people tend to dominate the project from the beginning.

But not so the industrial products. New-product projects more commonly arise and start their development in the research department or in one of the other technology-oriented corners of the company. Even if it passes from there to a "commercial development" group, that group is often technologically oriented. And often, in making their original profitability estimates, upon which the funding of the continuing development of the project depends, they ignore the very real costs (and time) involved in the introduction and initial marketing of the product. Thus when the time comes to allocate funds to the product-launching, there seems to be no real place to fit those costs without destroying the original profitability projections.

Whatever the background, however, the fact remains that we must determine the basic budget as a fundamental step in developing strategy. And this figure must lie somewhere between two basic amounts. We must provide more than the minimum necessary to bring the product before the public and less than that amount which will render the product completely profitless. For most projects the range between these two figures is wide enough so that the decision as to the budget allocation becomes a matter of judgment. Where communications costs are extremely high, however, the range may be narrow enough to make an analysis of both figures critical. And some products are doomed to failure because there is no room between the two figures.

A problem that often limits funding to an unrealistically low level is the need, felt by most companies, to limit the funding to what can be supplied from other company operations. While this sounds highly logical on the surface, it in effect makes the product's future dependent on factors totally unrelated to the product itself. Despite this, it is not uncommon for a product to have its launching budget cut significantly because of economic reverses in another line. And it is not uncommon for a new company, operating on venture capital, to outdistance a far better capitalized rival, because it stands ready to make the initial investment needed without being obliged (at least for a few years) to show a profit to its stockholders.

In deciding to invest in the new-product introduction at a compromise level, management, often without realizing the full significance, is also deciding to limit the product growth to a rate below the maximum achievable. And it is also making a decision to limit its potential losses. Depending on the extent of the limitation, it may also be requiring that the allocated dollars be spent with inordinate efficiency. For if a minimum dollar allocation is coupled with inefficiency of expenditure, the net effect may well be the same as underfunding the project.

From management's point of view, the decision as to the total resources to be made available for the new-product introduction must be made in the context of the resources available, alternate priorities for use of the resources, and the many other factors that face management in any such dollar-allocation decision. But they should balance these factors with the full knowledge of the effect of limiting funds for the new-product introduction—information that is often not sufficiently spelled out at the time the decision is made.

ALLOCATING THE BUDGET

Having determined the total investment of money and resources to be placed behind the introduction of the new product, the next strategic decision must relate to the allocation of this investment. How much of it will go to direct sales effort as compared to communications? How much should be spent for service and how much for physical distribution? Presumably the general allocations of comparable products in industries will have been studied, so some guidance will have been provided by this time as to the industry patterns for such an allocation.

Industry figures are valuable for guidance, of course, but the real strategic opportunity may well lie in a decision to allocate resources differently from the existing pattern—if such an allocation will truly be more efficient. For example, in an industry where advertising expenditures normally run at 15 percent of gross marketing expenditures, a decision might easily be made, and often is in the new-product-introduction phase, to upset that balance and put 50 percent of the marketing dollars toward advertising, and thus, in effect, reduce the funds available for direct selling expense. Or a decision might be made to forgo the establishment of a service organization and to provide a larger commission to distributors to cover their added cost of handling this service with the help of local service people. Or a decision might be made to concentrate expenditures on technical service aimed directly at the two or three largest buyers in the field.

Before making allocation decisions, it is important to have available as much information as possible about the patterns of allocation within the industry. But it is equally important to utilize that information only as a starting point from which to make creative deviations. To use it as a means by which to pattern yourself after the competition does reduce risk, but it also reduces the opportunity to move out ahead of the competition. In effect, it reduces the contest to a show of force, and if your investment decision leads you to a position where you have fewer dollars in the field than the competition, you can count on losing the battle.

MARKET POSITIONING

The next basic decision is the decision on market positioning. If sufficient resources are available, a company might try to enter a market on a broad front and get a maximum penetration in every market segment. But usually resources are limited. In order to get maximum return, we must concentrate our efforts on those segments of the market that will give us a disproportionately high return.

Selection of the area or areas to be attacked may or may not be obvious. The decision must be based not only on the size of the area selected, but the characteristics of the product. In developing the marketing-position strategy, we must look at the traditional market segmentation patterns as well as some of the nontraditional ones. We must look at the size of the various segments as well as the profitability and the market acceptance of the competing companies within those segments. And we must then decide where to concentrate our efforts. The decision may be to start the market penetration by making a heavy commitment toward one single market segment, by assigning priorities equally among three segments, or by assigning priorities among the same three segments in perhaps a 60/30/10 relationship.

Sometimes the market can be segmented in terms of buyer attitude rather than in terms of the more formal types of segmentation found in the usual statistical reports. For example, an industry may be filled with competitive suppliers who provide quality products, good technical service, and reasonable price and credit terms. Your market entry might simply be based on helping the customers sell their products, an area to which the existing supplier has paid no attention. Or you might want to build your position in an area of technology in which your company and its associated product have a clear superiority.

It is difficult to generalize on the kind of market-segmentation strategy that might be developed—the strategies are so dependent on the particular product situation and the particular market involved. Here, though, is the area where a maximum amount of creative thinking can be applied and where opportunity exists for almost any company—if it seeks it out.

Let us examine a few examples of how companies have entered markets with a market-segmentation strategy. When Du Pont first introduced Corfam®, synthetic leather material, it felt that it had a product that could compete with leather at almost any price range. But its initial strategy was to limit the sale to the high-priced, high-quality end of the market. It did this for two reasons: because its production capacity was limited in the early stages, and because it was felt that when production capacity was increased, penetration of the lower-priced markets would be facilitated if a quality reputation had already been developed. When Ciba-Geigy Corporation introduced a reflection densitometer (a quality-control instrument used in color printing) into the U.S. market, it recognized that its densitometer's improved features would broaden the market considerably. It would do this by winning over printers who used no such instrument because of the difficulties involved in getting accurate readings with existing instruments. The company's strategy was to make a rapid penetration into the segment of the market already using such an instrument before attempting to penetrate the unconverted segment of the market.

And there have been numerous cases—some successful, others not—where products were first aimed at the low-cost and unsophisticated segments of a market before being permitted to compete for the sophisticated segments.

THE RISK/BENEFIT RATIO

One of the most significant elements of new-product-introduction strategy, if not the most significant, is the establishment of the various policies in such a way as to increase the risk/benefit ratio of the product offering from the point of view of the buyer. His is the only point of view that determines market acceptance. We must always remember that the prospective buyer, in evaluating any product offering, is making an analysis of benefits and risks. To make a positive decision he must feel that the evaluation is weighted on the side of the benefit. In an industrial situation, the benefit can usually be reduced to one area—increase of profit for the user. This is most commonly provided by a reduction of cost, but not infrequently it can be provided by an increase in the selling price or the marketability of his own product. Even if the key benefit is convenience, or longer life, or better appearance, or reduction of the risk involved in continuing with his current system, or any similar "intangible" benefit, it can and must be reduced to its effect on the profitability structure of the product produced by the buyer, whether the buyer recognizes this consciously or not.

Risk, however, is a totally different type of consideration. Risk exists at two levels. One is the risk that the company feels it is taking in trying the new and untested product. The second is the risk that the individual within a company structure feels he is personally taking in making the decision in favor of the new product. These are very different types of risks, but they are of equal importance, and both must be dealt with.

The term "product offering," referred to earlier, was used advisedly. It is not the same as the product. Rather, it includes product, price, credit terms, service, contractual obligations, end-market communications, reciprocal buying obligations, use restriction, and any other additions or limitations the seller places on the product purchase. In a very real sense, the product offering is a manifestation of many of the strategic and tactical decisions made to support the new product.

The risk involved in using a new product is very different for different product classes. A manufacturer of fabricated metal products accepts a certain number of risks when he changes his source of supply of a basic mill product. He protects himself against most product risks by setting specifications for the material. He protects himself from supplier performance risks by splitting his business during the transition. If either the supplier or the material fails to perform properly, he may lose a small amount of production or he may have to make some adjustments in his own plant to utilize the less-than-satisfactory material. But since these risks are relatively small, for a similarly small savings in raw-material cost, he will normally decide in favor of a new supplier.

On the other hand, a manufacturer of precision ball bearings might be buying $100 worth of rust preventative to protect $100,000 worth of bearings. If you offer him an alternative rust preventative at half the price, or for nothing, or even pay him to take it, it will still require a great deal of persuasion to get him to risk the total value of his precision-made parts for the small dollar benefits that you are offering.

Such an objective risk analysis from the point of view of the customer company is only one piece of the risk consideration, however. A key element of the analysis is how the buyer perceives the risks. This may or may not be consistent with the actual risk involved.

The difference between actual risk and perceived risk (and to a lesser degree the difference between absolute benefit and perceived benefit) arises from two factors—first, the information level of the buyer, and second, his ability to evaluate that information. Coping with any deficiencies in the information level is a normal objective of the marketing communication program. But improving the ability of the buyer to evaluate the risk or benefit is a totally different thing. It might become part of the communications strategy, conceivably, or introduction might instead concentrate on bypassing the need entirely.

What most commonly affects the buyer's ability to evaluate both risk and benefit is his educational and experience background, the factors that principally determine his sophistication in a given technological area. Thus a piece of new computer equipment produced by a brand new company may look very positive on the risk/benefit ratio scale to a sophisticated data processing manager, whose experience level permits him to understand the real benefits. But when he asks for an appropriation, he may find that the ratio looks completely the opposite to those who must approve the request, who may never have heard of any other supplier but IBM. Similarly, a chemical-process engineer may feel very comfortable in selecting a new corrosion-resistant material on the basis of his knowledge of the projectability of corrosion tests. Top management, faced with the responsibility of getting a return on the total plant investment, may see a far greater risk in using an untried material.

As indicated before, risk to an individual must be looked at separately from risk to a company. A hospital purchasing agent will suffer great embarrassment if he ever runs out of anything, whether important or not, because of the particularly stratified pecking order that exists within the medical-services field. A strategy for penetrating this market must emphasize the minimal risk to any member of the hospital staff of being placed in a position where he might suffer disapproval on the part of a doctor. Similarly, an engineer may be putting his career in jeopardy if he recommends a major innovation that turns out a disaster. He too will want to be reassured in the matter of risk.

Individual risk as well as company risk are both related to the position that the new product fills within the buying company. When a man buys a piece of auxiliary equipment and it functions poorly, his embarrassment can be ended by simply replacing that piece of equipment. If on the other hand, the equipment he buys should be in the heart of the company's production system, a failure to perform can affect total plant performance and call down on him the wrath of production people, salespeople, and even general management. Similarly, any new product that calls for a change in operating procedures in order to utilize its special benefits puts the people who recommend the change in particular jeopardy. Any difficulty encountered with the new product affects all the groups that have been involved in the change, many of whom probably predicted such failure during the early deliberations.

It is important that this personal risk to the individual be recognized in developing strategy, especially in areas where many other people will be affected by the decision to use the new product. Either the benefits of the product must be so great that the key individual involved will be willing to stick his neck out, or something in the product offering must protect him against the contingency of failure. This protection might be provided by a guarantee, or assurance of back-up service, or perhaps by a price structure scaled to the efficiency of the new unit. The last is common practice in the purchase of power-plant equipment, where the price is related to the efficiency of the equipment, as measured after installation.

It is difficult, of course, to project a risk/benefit analysis based on a buyer's knowledge level and vantage point within a company to an entire market. But the new-product manager must establish his product offering and his communications program for an entire market segment rather than for a single prospect. What looks like a low risk/benefit ratio to one company may look like a high one to another because of its own particular production setup or accounting technique. And even within a single company, what looks like a low ratio to one of the buying influences may look high to another.

One of the keys to new-product-introduction strategy is to modify the perceived risk/benefit ratio to the point where it will look favorable to a sufficient number of buyers to support the production of the product at profitable levels. Sometimes this can be done by adjusting the price downward, a factor that by itself can significantly increase the benefits to the buyer. But this, of course, lowers the profit margins too. More often the key to new-product-introduction strategy is to devise techniques that lower the risk for a large segment of the buying public without adding too greatly to the costs of the seller. Whether this is done by providing a "guarantee," or by simplifying the sampling and testing procedures, or by establishing and communicating the service available, or by educating buyers to a better understanding of the real risks involved, or by a different and completely innovative strategy approach, is unimportant. The important thing is that the risk/benefit ratio as perceived by the bulk of the buyers be moved toward a favorable decision for the new product.

PRICING AND TERMS

Unquestionably, one of the most significant strategy decisions for any product is the setting of the price along with the accompanying price structure and terms. Price policy is significant not only to profitability, but also to the decision on market-segmentation strategy, for nothing will move a product away from a particular segment of a market faster than a price structure that that segment cannot justify. Frequently, different price structures have to be established for different market segments. The basic price decided upon, its relation to competitive prices, and its relation to the prices of alternate ways of accomplishing the same thing, will all have a very heavy bearing on the speed of market penetration in each market segment.

A great deal has been written about the pricing of products, and this book will not attempt to duplicate the many volumes that should rate space in the decision maker's library. Most such references probe in depth such things as the elasticity of demand as related to price, analysis of the retaliatory capability of competitors, optimization of profits, and so on. But most of them assume a static marketing situation rather than the dynamic one that surrounds a new-market entry. Even with this drawback, basic pricing theory is probably well worth study by the new-product manager since it is one of the pillars upon which he must build his pricing decision. In the dynamic world of new-product introduction, though, the pricing factor that is rarely covered in the standard texts, the application of risk/benefit ratio analysis, must be given equal weight.

As pointed out earlier, a fundamental objective of many strategy decisions is to move the risk/benefit ratio as perceived by a significant segment of the prospective buying influences to a level that will invite purchase of the new product. While risks can be reduced by a variety of techniques, reduced price or easy credit terms are the most common techniques for increasing the benefit part of the equation.

Though the basic price of the product is an important element, it is not the only one involved in pricing strategy. For mechanical equipment, pricing strategy also includes the pricing pattern for options and for parts or supplies that must be used with the equipment. Marketing people have for years been talking about "giving away the razor so we can sell the blades." Such pricing practices are not unknown in the industrial field. Office copiers that require special papers are only one example.

Pricing patterns for options offer similar strategic pricing opportunities. A computer company recently introduced a product with what seemed an impossibly low basic price. The price offering itself bought the company a great deal of publicity and recognition. But what was offered was in essence a stripped-down version almost unusable without options. With the options the buyers needed, the price, while still low, was at least within range of competitive offerings. Others in the same business have offered complete units with the option of reducing the price if some of the segments were not to be purchased. Neither strategy is correct—or wrong—per se.

Each was designed to fit a particular situation and to enhance the product's initial marketability in the segment of the market sought by the manufacturer.

Credit terms are another policy area that should not be left to chance. Worse still, they should not be applied in exactly the same way as for the company's past products, especially if the new product is to be sold to a different industrial segment. Often strategic application of credit policies can make the difference between fast or slow penetration of an industrial market. If the industry involved is growing very rapidly, it is also likely to be capital-hungry. In such a market, providing extended credit terms for your product can often make a greater difference in its acceptability than lowering its price.

DISTRIBUTION PATTERNS

Distribution patterns can be divided into two major areas of strategic decision. The first relates to the type and structure of the selling organization that will carry the product message on a person-to-person basis and negotiate the purchase details. The second lies in the area of physical distribution decisions.

The first group, the decisions relating to who will carry the product message and serve as liaison between the supplier company and the buying company, is usually the area that requires the greatest amount of care. Physical distribution policies—the policies relating to inventory, warehousing, and other physical movement of goods—while equally important, and perhaps more so for certain products, are not generally as hard to establish. The reason is that the types of products that demand special attention to the physical distribution system are probably obvious in that need.

Distribution Channels

The key question relating to the channels of distribution is normally whether to sell the product directly through company salesmen or whether to use manufacturers' representatives or distributors. Of course the possibility of using both patterns in selected territories can also be considered. Where a company has existing sales patterns for other products, the considerations go beyond structure to the question of whether or not to use the present organization, whichever type it may be.

The alternatives are many, and the advantages-disadvantages analysis of each type of selling organization is normally loaded with pros and cons for every option.

For existing products the company normally has two major objectives that it wants to see met in establishing its channel of distribution. It wants to set up a system that will provide the maximum of sales, while at the same time it wants a system that will provide the lowest cost of selling per unit sold. These same two criteria exist, of course, in a new-product situation, but a third and often more important one is added. That is that the selling organization must be in place in the shortest possible amount of time. The decisions based on the first two criteria are often quite simple. The third variable is what often makes the decisions on distribution patterns for new products difficult.

Where the new product fits into a market already being served by a company, the decision is normally quite easy to make. Not only has the existing sales and distribution pattern been tested over a period of time as the most effective pattern with the lowest cost for that company, but the new product can probably be moved into the existing sales organization in the minimum amount of time. And with so many other factors that demand change when a new product begins to fight for commercial life, this is certainly the last area where one ought to try to innovate. Care should be taken of course to make sure that the organization can absorb an additional workload, and that the salesmen have sufficient incentive to devote time to the new product. And of course, existing incentives for existing products should be looked at carefully to make sure that none of them might deter the salesman from putting his efforts behind the new product.

For example, if an existing internal sales force has an incentive related to gross volume, the introduction of a new product that provides fewer dollars but equal or higher profits to the company will be inconsistent with the salesmen's personal objectives. The compensation plan must be modified accordingly, or the new product will be ignored by the salesmen. And if sales contests are under way based on short-term performance, neither direct nor distributor salesmen will look kindly on the idea of spending their time on a new product, even if they are convinced of its long-term sales potential. With these objections taken care of, however, by special incentives, by sales training, by compensation systems, or even by strong direction by management, the existing sales force and sales pattern are normally the best ones to use in this type of situation.

On the other hand, if the new product serves a market partly or totally different from that now being served by the company, the direction of the final decision can go almost anywhere. An established sales force, currently organized to serve other markets, might be utilized, as long as the salesmen are given proper instruction in how to serve the market toward which the new product is being aimed. Or a new sales force can be hired. Or a network of manufacturers' representatives might be set up. Or a network of distributors might be organized.

While no recommendation can be made out of the context of a specific situation, it would be well to look at each one of these situations and explore advantages and disadvantages.

Alternative 1—Utilize the Existing Company Salesmen

The technique of utilizing salesmen already with the company has the advantage of providing people of known capability in an existing organization structure, so that no delay is encountered in creating an effective organization. Little or no additional front-end investment is needed to put new salesmen on the staff.

Using the existing sales organization has the disadvantage, however, that the productivity of such a sales group is less predictable than is generally assumed. It usually takes longer than most people judge necessary for the salesmen to adapt themselves to new markets. Being unfamiliar with these markets, they are slower to bring back realistic appraisals of new-product effectiveness from the point of view of the buyers. And being human, and therefore tending to put a higher priority on the things at which they are most proficient, they will often put the new and difficult calls on the bottom of their priority list while they continue to serve familiar markets. And obviously, if they invest the time necessary to move the new product into the new market, this will reduce the time they can spend on the established product lines in their established markets. Thus a conflict of interest inevitably results. Some salesmen can handle it well, others cannot. In examining the pros and cons, what we often find is that using an existing sales force to support a new-product–new-market area always seems to promise the fastest and most efficient way of establishing a selling organization. And there are times when it does work out that way. But as often as not, the advantages of establishing the sales force in this manner represent pure illusion, and the time it is hoped will be saved turns into time irrevocably lost.

In deciding whether or not the use of an existing structure makes sense for a particular organization, the project manager should look carefully at the reasons behind that structure. Any sales organization, whether it is an internal company sales force or a distributor or manufacturers' representative company, is organized around three basic parameters: products, markets, and geographic territories.

A sales force segmented on the basis of specific products will comprise a group of people who are well versed in the product and who can therefore communicate its selling points accurately and efficiently to prospective customers. A sales force specializing by market will have a high degree of knowledge of the particular market that the product serves and therefore will be able to act quickly and efficiently in seeing that the product fits the specific needs of the potential customer. A sales force segmented by geographic territory can make frequent calls on prospective customers with a minimum of lost time and travel expense. Thus the ideal sales force would be broken down by geographic territory with specialists for each market area and specialists for each product area within each of these marketing selling units. However, there are few, if any, products that can support the number of people who would be involved in such a sales force.

To provide a balance between the needs of marketing and the available capital, compromise is always necessary. Some companies find it worthwhile to structure the sales organization according to product lines, with each salesman handling a

single product group in a variety of markets. Thus each salesman can develop a high level of product knowledge which he
then applies to the various markets to which he sells the product. Perhaps a group of staff market specialists work with him
in special problems relating to certain of his markets.

Other companies assign their salesmen according to
markets, with each salesman handling a number of products.
Thus each salesman becomes highly knowledgeable in the
needs of his particular market and develops sufficient product
know-how to help carry the product message. Frequently, the
product managers operating on a staff basis will help him
where needed.

Many companies organize their sales forces along geographic lines. This of course helps keep the cost and time
involved in moving from customer to customer to a reasonable
level. The salesman will then know his territory from a geographic point of view, but he still must serve various markets
with various products.

What most companies end up with is some sort of hybrid
organization designed to provide the greatest effectiveness for
the least cost. Thus a company with a basically geographic
breakdown of sales territories may have product specialists or
market specialists located within some of the larger territories
but not in the smaller ones. And a single product line with a
very small number of customers might be handled directly by
one or two product people who travel extensively. Another
company will put two or three product lines together for
handling by one sales force, while another product line may
be handled independently. Another might segregate its own
salesmen by geographic territory and utilize manufacturers'
agents and distributors to handle the specific markets for the
product within each of those territories.

Each such structure is normally developed over a long

period of time with a great deal of trial and error in its development. When a new product is put into this structure, however, there is no reason to believe that the organization will remain optimal for the new product's needs. Usually one of two things will happen. Either the structure will remain intact and reject the new product (or simply handle it badly), or the structure will reorient itself around the new product in combination with the old. It is extremely difficult in the early stages of new-product-strategy development to know which will happen. But a study of the product, market, and geographic breakdown of a company's products will provide the kind of guidance that can tell the project manager whether assignment of the new product to an existing sales force is likely to be the wise decision.

Alternative 2—Establish a New Direct Sales Organization

A common solution to the sales organization problem in a new-product–new-market situation is the decision to form a whole new sales organization. Because one can build a staff with people who are knowledgeable in the marketplace, it is possible to obtain a more efficient use of time in the earlier stages simply because such a staff knows which companies are likely to buy and whom to see there. Their feedback to the design and production people is likely to be far more accurate and far more reflective of the market point of view than similar reports from a sales force unsophisticated in the market. Such a sales force can therefore make a valuable contribution in correcting certain product and market-policy decisions before they carry the introduction too far off course.

The disadvantages to this approach, however, are many. The time lag in hiring salesmen, establishing them in their physical locations, training them in the company way of doing things, and overcoming their personal problems in relating to a new environment is usually far greater than any company dares to estimate in its preliminary planning. Combine this with the attrition rate normally involved in hiring any group of people, and the average company will find that within six months or a year, somewhere between 25 percent and 50 percent of its early hires will no longer be around. With all these factors, a company rarely finds that it has an effective new sales force in place in anything less than a year's time.

Another basic disadvantage of an inside sales force is that it requires a significant investment in salaries, overhead, and facilities before sales levels rise to the point where the sales staff can be supported. Not only is the front-end investment high, but the company is committed to a relatively high and inflexible overhead, which may or may not be supportable by the product. If the product is successful, this course will probably prove to have been the wisest decision, but if the product proves unsuccessful the losses will be that much higher. And if the product proves only moderately successful, the overhead might make the difference between moderate success and failure.

This is not to say that the disadvantages of establishing a new direct sales force for a new-product–new-market situation far outweigh the advantages. For many situations this is probably the most productive course of action. But the project manager should recognize that the establishment of a direct selling force for a new product is a front-end investment decision in the same sense that product development and manufacturing tooling are front-end decisions. This approach will normally increase the chances of success but it will also increase the losses if the new product fails.

Alternative 3—Use Manufacturers' Representatives

When a company is introducing a new product into a new market, it often looks to the establishment of a manufacturer's-representative network as the optimum approach. A manufacturer's representative is an independent company, often comprising only one individual, serving a variety of accounts in a particular market. He sells these products for his principals on a commission basis. For the company with a new product, the establishment of a "rep" organization has the advantage that, without a front-end investment or an overhead commitment of any kind, it can add to the staff people who are knowledgeable in the market, have day-to-day selling connections with it, and who are located in the right geographic areas. The arrangements can be "turned on" very quickly too, a factor extremely important for a new product.

The principal disadvantage is that the cost of selling this way often is higher than the equivalent cost of direct company salesmen. Also, if the representative proves ineffective in a territory, or unwilling to devote his time to the product, it is usually difficult and time-consuming to break off the relationship and locate a new group who can properly serve the territory.

To be obliged to work through a manufacturer's representative, who sometimes has his own set of salesmen, will mean a whole new level of communications barriers between the company and the buyer of the product. These barriers are often great enough that company selling policies are difficult to apply through the communications chain, and accurate feedback from the customer to the supplying company becomes more the exception than the rule. And the interposing of a separate business organization into the chain of communication and selling puts incentives into the hands of salesmen that are often not consistent with the direction that the corporation wants to go in.

The manufacturer's representative and his salesmen normally have to deal with multiple demands for their time. This, coupled with the difficulties in communications, outlined above, give valuable guidance to the type of product for which they can provide the greatest amount of assistance. Where products are firmly established in their design and are therefore moved to customers on an "as offered" basis, the manufacturer's representative can be extremely valuable. Where the product is such that some handling must be done for each individual application, thus requiring clear customer-supplier communications as a step to each sale, the manufacturer's representative is normally far less effective. Where the characteristics fall somewhere between, as they do so frequently, a judgment must be made as to the potential effectiveness of a manufacturer's representative type of selling organization.

An alternative to a manufacturer's representative is the use of distributors, or wholesalers, as they are often called. These organizations are similar to manufacturers' representatives where new products are concerned, except that where the manufacturer's representative never takes legal possession of the goods, the distributor does. The distributor may stock the goods for local distribution, or he may simply pass on orders from his customers to the principal company. Either way, however, he comes into legal possession of the goods before they go to the customer. Thus the wholesaler serves such functions as supplying small-quantity customers with small-quantity shipments and accepting credit risks, neither of which the manufacturer's representative will do. Beyond that, their functions are essentially the same, and the advantages and disadvantages of working with the two organizations are similar, except that the distributor normally carries far more products than the manufacturer's representative, and thus can be expected to give the new product even less of his time.

A large number of companies find that to enter a new market area with a new product, the use of manufacturers' representatives or distributor organizations, with all their disadvantages, is frequently the most efficient way of starting the distribution pattern. If this is combined with special communications efforts to circumvent the problems caused by the added levels of management and the number of people interposed between the supplier and the buyer, and if the project manager moves rapidly in dropping and replacing ineffective representatives, this technique offers one of the best compromise choices for many products.

Often it seems logical to start the distribution of a new product through a representative or distributor type of sales organization, to be replaced later, when the product is established, by direct company salesmen. This limits the financial risks at the front end before the product is proved, and it probably offers a faster entry into the market than would result from establishing a direct sales organization at the beginning.

The representatives and distributors are well aware of such strategies, however, and are constantly wary of going to great efforts to build up a market that is later going to be taken away from them by the principals. Their contracts are written in such a way that they are difficult to terminate, and they often keep the customer relationships so secretive that if the principal does adopt that type of policy in the future, he can still maintain the customer relationship with another competitive principal.

Such a strategy can be used in introducing new products, and it may be sound for many kinds of products, but where it is considered, the project manager should bear in mind that the transition is a lengthy, expensive, and sometimes traumatic step, and one that should not be undertaken lightly.

Physical-Distribution Policies

The second major element in the distribution pattern is the area known as physical distribution. This has been defined as "movement and handling of goods from the point of production to the point of consumption." In general, this term includes such functions as inventory control, warehousing, and transportation of the product. As a general rule, physical-distribution policies are set up to balance two factors. The first is aimed at keeping the cost of movement of the goods to the lowest possible level. The second is aimed at providing the customers with the kind of delivery service they need and expect. For products such as major machinery that has to be custom-engineered and custom-delivered, there is no real problem in fixing physical-distribution policy other than that the best routes of transportation be sought. For commodity products that serve as ingredients for other products, or for components of other manufacturers' products, the physical-distribution structure must be organized to allow for the needs and ordering patterns of the user industries.

Usually, the physical-distribution pattern required of a new product will become apparent from a study of the market and from a study of the physical-distribution patterns of competitive companies. It is only where a look at existing patterns points toward either an inefficiency or a failure to fully meet customer needs that physical-distribution innovation can become a part of a company's new-product-introduction strategy.

An example. If, in the basic study of a market, one learns that West Coast customers have to place their orders further in advance than is justified by their own sales-forecasting techniques, introductory strategy for a new product might call for immediate establishment of a warehouse on the West Coast from which shipments can be made overnight. The cost of such a strategy must be looked at carefully, as the competitor's ability to retaliate must be looked at, but in the proper economic situation, this can be a viable strategy for developing rapid initial market penetration. Or if a study of the market indicates that there exists an elaborate and expensive distribution network that was set up by competing companies for an earlier time when such service was important, one might set up a strategy calling for limited distribution facilities and a price structure aimed at the bigger buying companies that would offer significant discounts and make possible large direct shipments at lower costs for companies willing to do some advance planning.

The opportunities for using physical-distribution innovation as a key to marketing strategy are few and far between, but where they do exist they can be effective in promoting rapid market penetration for a new product.

SERVICE POLICIES

The service policies related to the new product can similarly prove to be a key element in a new-product-introduction strategy. Though the term "service" has somewhat different meanings for different kinds of businesses, the types of activities referred to are often the same. In the mechanical-equipment business, "service" relates to installation, repair, and at times the initial tune-up of equipment as it is installed in the customer's plant. Here the primary emphasis of service is on keeping the equipment in repair. In the case of components or ingredient-type products, the term "service" normally refers to the technical assistance provided at the customer level to better enable the customer to utilize the product. This might include help in modifying the customer's equipment or modifying the process involved to enable him to use the new product effectively, as well as solving processing problems once the material is in use. In either case, service is built around a staff of engineers and technicians who perform at the customer-use location rather than at the point of production.

Technical service, whatever its type, is extremely expensive. It calls for the training and the maintenance on staff of a number of highly skilled people who must be capable of providing the kind of service needed in the field. The key strategic decisions on the part of the project manager relate to how much technical service capability he must provide, how he is going to handle it, and whether part of the cost might be borne by the customer. Within this decision must be balanced the needs of the customer, the availability of financial and manpower resources, and the effect of the service policies on the risk/benefit ratio.

For most products the minimum level of technical service that must be provided is determined either by patterns already in existence within the industry, or by the specific needs of the product. For relatively simple equipment that can be repaired by any skilled mechanic, the minimum amount of technical service required is the preparation of a good instruction manual that can be followed in the field. Or the usual 30-, or 60-, or 90-day guarantee against defects in materials and workmanship, coupled with a replacement policy for defective goods, may be sufficient. But for a complex, customized piece of production machinery, such as a printing press or paper machine, the minimum may require putting an engineer or a technician or both at the customer's plant for a two- or three-month start-up period.

If the new product is a material that is usable under different conditions from those previously encountered in the field, it will be almost impossible to market without technical assistance to the customer to guide him in proper use of the material. In the introduction of a new plastic breadwrap film that had narrower temperature limitations than had been encountered with existing breadwrap materials, it became necessary for the supplier to modify the customer's machinery-control systems before the latter could use the new material. And many companies selling ingredients for adhesives or paints or other chemical specialties have found that they must help the customer reformulate his product in order to make a sale.

The maximum of technical service that might be provided is something totally different. In the case of heavy equipment, a company may want to offer production-line redesign and foundation design as an additional service in selling its product—usually to eliminate the resistance on the part of potential customers to undertaking these activities themselves. In the materials business, suppliers commonly offer technical service to their customers that is essentially a technical consulting service, at no charge to the customer.

How broad to make such a technical-service offering and at what point to start charging customers for such service are key strategy decisions. The best way to arrive at the optimum decision is to first look at the patterns that exist in the industry, and to look upon them as minimums. To support the added cost of going beyond them, the risk/benefit ratio must be so adjusted by this as to make the product more salable, and the market more quickly penetrable—at a cost that can be supported by the product potential.

A second strategic decision relating to technical service is the organization of the technical-service function. Does an internal technical-service staff have to be organized and a support facility established? Or can satisfactory service be provided through existing independent service organizations? If an internal staff is set up, should it be centralized or decentralized?

Some of these considerations may be considered tactical rather than strategic in that, once the level of technical service to be provided and the accompanying price policy has been decided, the organization needed to carry it out will be a matter of tactical detail. There are many situations, however, in which technical service can become a strategic decision—namely, when it weighs heavily in the perceived risk/benefit ratio analysis. If the new product's continuing operation is essential to the operations of the customer, the speed of service that you will supply and the believability that that service will be provided will be significant factors in the product offering—often more significant than who pays the cost of the service.

For example, a piece of sterilization or bottling equipment for a dairy cannot be out of service for more than a few hours. A piece of malfunctioning communications gear in a computer system can make the rest of the system inoperable.

In these and many other similar situations, the manner in which the service is organized and the credibility you inspire as to the availability of such service can be key factors in product acceptance.

COMMUNICATIONS STRATEGY

The communications approach is one of the most significant strategy decisions to be made in a new-product introduction. Not only must a decision be made as to the total dollars to be invested in communications, but decisions must be made as to how to distribute the investment and toward what communications objectives. Since the start of a communications program is the key area in crossing the line between product development and product commercialization, the communications strategy occupies a key role.

But communications strategy is also one of the least independent of the strategy considerations. If we look at the new-product-introduction step as making public the product offering, it becomes apparent that the objective of communications is largely to carry the message of the other strategic decisions to the projected audiences. Thus many of the elements that are normally considered part of communications strategy are predetermined by the strategies already decided upon for the product. For example, the decision on pricing and terms will have a major effect on communications objectives. And the marketing positioning and segmentation strategy will provide direct guidance to the kind of media strategy that will be needed. If a decision is made to concentrate on the biggest companies in the field, one type of communications program will be needed. If a decision is made to narrow the introduction to one segment of the market, another type will be needed. The decision on total financial support to be given the product introduction is an important one in guiding communications strategy, since communications costs are commonly a highly significant portion of the product-introduction expense.

Though tied to the other strategy elements, the communications strategy decisions should not be made after them, but in conjunction with them. The other important decisions should always be made with full consideration for the communications pattern likely to evolve. For example, a decision on total dollar allocation and market-segmentation policies could easily be inconsistent with the amount needed to communicate effectively with those segments of the markets. Similarly, in selecting a trade name, the question of how well it can be communicated should be kept in mind. Again, price policy on options might be determined by whether or not that policy can be stated in a single line in an advertisement. And the technique of distribution decided upon will determine what proportion of the communications dollars are needed to support the distributing organization. A system of manufacturers' agents and distributors will require that a far greater percentage of the communications budget be allocated to internal communications than one in which a direct sales organization is utilized. Thus it is important that communications strategy be developed in tandem with all other related decisions so that the final total strategic package is completely harmonious.

Though many communications-strategy decisions, such as total expenditures, definition of audience, and distribution of funds between objectives, are largely dictated by other strategic decisions and therefore are more properly tactical, a certain number of truly strategic decisions still must be made. Most of these lie in the area of objective-setting. The key questions that must be asked before communications dollars are spent are these: "What is it that we want the people we reach to do? Do we want them to simply absorb the information as a preliminary to a call by a salesman? Do we want them to respond if they have a small degree of interest so they can be followed up in the future? Do we want them to identify themselves and provide enough data so that we can evaluate their potential and determine where the sales manpower can best be invested? Do we want them to come to a demonstration location and see the new product in operation? Do we merely want to reduce some resistance to the new product that might be in their minds? Or do we want to educate them in the technology involved to a point where they can more reliably evaluate the risks and benefits of the new product, and thereby close the gap between actual risk/benefit ratio and the perceived ratio?" The amount of funds needed to do all of these things will probably never be available for any new-product introduction ever. So the real strategic decisions involve the question of which one or two or perhaps three objectives can be expected to give us the greatest return for our investment in communications dollars.

For a large number of new-product introductions the strategic communications approach is quite straightforward. The objective is to bring in inquiries so as to identify people who have some interest in the product. These inquiries are then screened, and those with the greatest degree of interest in the product are given maximum attention. This is the strategy followed in probably 80 percent of new-product introductions. Still, this is not always the most productive strategy. For a major piece of equipment with a number of unusual features, it might be best to set up demonstrations of the equipment and to use mass communications to bring people to the demonstration. For a product that involves a totally new concept, it might be best to run technical seminars to educate people to the level where they can understand the concept behind the utilization of the new product, and mass communications should be utilized to bring people to the seminars and communicate once they are gathered. If the new product is directly competitive with something already on the market it might prove best to communicate strongly the one or two key differences in the product offering and solicit information as to who in the audience has the specific kind of problems that your marketing strategy is designed to solve.

Frequently, the inquiry-development type of strategy can be used as the first step of a program that calls for following up with a concept-communication type of strategy. Not infrequently, a new product's market consists of a relatively limited number of individuals who are highly sophisticated in the technology involved, plus a far larger number of potential buyers who have to be schooled in the technology or in the acceptance of a new system before they can be considered true prospects. A common strategy for this situation is to first use a straight features-oriented communications program designed to obtain inquiries from the small and sophisticated portion of the market, people who can understand a product's benefits through a description of its features.

After an initial first-phase communications thrust aimed at the smaller segment of the market, there can begin the larger, benefits-oriented, program, directed to the group of people not immediately familiar with the product benefits. While both kinds of programs could be begun simultaneously, where funds are limited it makes sense to first obtain the efficiency benefits of communicating to the sophisticates in the market, and then use the profits derived from that group to help support the communications program directed to the broader segment of the market.

One of the key areas of communications strategy lies in evaluating the tradeoffs between the strength of the message and the desire to reach the number of people who have to be reached. Within the limits of available funds, decisions have to be made as to whether marketing objectives can best be met with a communications program that makes a strong impact on a small number of people or with one that makes a weaker impression on a larger group. This usually comes down to the questions of how big a space unit to use for advertising, what the frequency of advertising will be in each publication selected, how many publications will be used in a given field, and how many fields will be covered. The decision might even cut across types of media, however, and be at the heart of the decision to use direct mail as the key medium instead of space.

The "impact" versus "reach" question must be decided on the basis of judgments as to how much persuasion it will take to move a prospect to action. If the product is one whose benefits are immediately recognizable to a large number of people, and the strategy calls for getting the largest number of inquiries, it probably makes sense to try to reach the largest number of people through the widest variety of media. On the other hand, if the product is a sophisticated one, one that will probably require a certain amount of persuasion before a prospect is ready to identify himself or to take action, communications strategy probably should call for advertising in large, dynamic space units, repeated frequently in a small number of publications that can efficiently reach that audience. This might prove to be only one publication. Or the marketing message might even be reduced to direct mail to known prospective buyers.

People in the advertising field frequently talk about creative media strategy, but this author sees few opportunities beyond tactical ones in this area. Once the other strategic communications decisions are made, and the audience is clearly defined, the selection of the media becomes a tactical exercise aimed at finding the most effective media mix for reaching the people described. In rare cases, a decision to use an unusual medium such as radio, television, or billboards for an industrial product might be looked upon as a creative strategy, but if it works well, as it sometimes does, it is probably because that medium was simply more efficient than was apparent from available data.

The real exception to this may well be those situations where the effectiveness of the message communication relates to the type of medium used, to the extent that it can overcome a relative inefficiency in the medium itself. For example, a fire-alarm system might be better introduced through radio than on the printed page simply because radio can more effectively carry the message. In the rare cases where such opportunities exist, they can certainly be considered creative strategy rather than tactical execution. Perhaps a few examples will more dramatically show some of the things that can create an effective communications strategy for a new-product introduction.

A company that introduced a new piece of electronic control equipment, for which it sought application in a wide variety of mechanically oriented industries, had its own salesmen, backed by distributor setup, already in place. Strategy called for a broad communication of the availability of the item in order to draw a substantial number of inquiries. This was followed by a program of screening the inquiries to select the real prospects among them, and forwarding the screened inquiries to the sales force and the distributor organization. With that strategy established, it became apparent that broad use of publicity was called for, backed up with space advertising in the more horizontal-inquiry-oriented journals. A sophisticated inquiry-handling system was of course a necessary part of the communications program.

A new polyethylene blow-molding resin was introduced that could take the place of two types of resins then being used in the field. Because its advantages were only to the plastic-bottle manufacturer, not to the final buyer, strategy called for direct communications to the known buyers of this type of plastic. Since there were only a few hundred manufacturers, most of them fairly small companies, direct mail and sales-assistance materials became the key elements in the communications program.

A sophisticated and expensive instrument was introduced. It involved a new concept in technology and a new business area for the company. A new sales force had to be built, so only a relatively small number of salesmen were available to support the introduction. The communications noise level in the field was very high, and a large number of other instruments seemed to lay claim to the same capabilities. Introduction strategy called for demonstrating the unit at a series of locations. Communications strategy therefore called for using local media to invite people to the demonstrations. This was combined with direct-mail invitations, plus advertising in regional editions of the publications serving the industry.

There are as many communications strategies as there are new-product-introduction strategies. In many cases the communications strategy is an obvious outgrowth of the marketing and production strategy. In others the market-introduction strategy blends into the communications strategy. Whichever way it works, it is important that they work together, for, fundamentally, new-product introduction is largely a communications function.

4

Mass Communications

In an earlier chapter we defined the new-product launching as the point of time at which the buying public becomes fully aware of a product's availability. Two basic types of routes are available to a company for use in communicating to its audiences the benefits, the risks, and the information needed by the buyer to understand these benefits and risks. These two routes are mass-communications techniques and direct contact. In this chapter we will look at the various impersonal mass-communications techniques that are normally used for carrying the product message to its audience. In the next we will look at the ways in which salesmen and other direct-contact personnel can be supported so as to improve their efficiency in carrying these messages.

A wide variety of mass-communications techniques can be used to support a new-product introduction. These include publicity, advertising, direct mail, literature, exhibits, demonstrations, movies, and a variety of "advertising" techniques for communication to broad audiences. Each of these areas has developed a sufficient body of know-how to support a full-length book. And indeed, books on most of these areas, and on most combinations, have been written. In general, these deal with specific "how to" information, presented in such a way as to assist the professional advertising manager as well as the practitioner in each of the subsegment communications disciplines to better practice his trade. This discussion, however, will be limited to the applicability of each communications technique to the introduction of new products. This is done on the assumption that the new-product project manager has available, either within his company or in an outside advertising agency, people with detailed knowledge of each of the communications techniques. If this is not the case, he had best make an arrangement with an advertising agency, rather than try to serve as his own communications professional.

PUBLICITY

"Publicity" is a broad term that includes a variety of subtechniques for utilizing the editorial pages of publications to carry the product message. The reader may be surprised that publicity appears before advertising as one of the mass-communications techniques. This is an unusual sequence, but the reason for it is that, in a new-product introduction, publicity normally plays the most important role in carrying the product message to the maximum number of people for the minimum cost in the shortest period of time. Normally publicity can be obtained in far more publications than the company can possibly afford to advertise in. And such stories generally get more readership and greater believability than can be obtained from advertising. New products are news. The entry of a company into a new market is news. The entry of a new company into an existing product area is news. And the business and trade publications that serve our industrial community thrive on news. This is so important to editors that in a market area served by an aggressive and dynamic press, a company will often be faced with leaks about the new product before it is ready to make its formal announcement.

Professional publicity men, or as they are sometimes called, public relations practitioners, use a variety of techniques to make certain that their product will be given the best possible treatment in the press. The most common and most fundamental publicity technique is the issuance of a press release. This is a simple written announcement distributed to the interested press announcing the product and describing its basic advantages and disadvantages along with other key information.

If the product promises to be significant to the industry, a press conference might be called for. There, a number of editors will hear a presentation on the new product and perhaps see a demonstration of it as well. The news release, of course, plays a part in the press conference, for it is important that written material be given to the newsmen to serve as source material for the stories they will write. Otherwise some gross inaccuracies might appear that would interfere with, rather than help, the product-communications program. The written material is usually provided in the form of a press kit. A typical press kit for a new-product press conference would include an announcement news release, a background sheet describing the nature of the problem that is being solved by the new product, some background on the company, a list of people who are attending the press conference, several pictures that the publications can use to dress up their stories, and perhaps a second or third news release featuring particular aspects of the new-product story.

It is important that the new-product manager judge carefully and objectively the significance of the new product to the market before he decides to call a press conference. Nothing is more disappointing to an editor than to attend a press conference that fails to provide him with what he considers a worthwhile story. We must always keep in mind that the editor must receive a satisfactory return for the time he invests in any activity, including a press conference. If the conference fails to provide him with the kind of material he needs for his story, your product is more likely to get negative than positive publicity. And your efforts to obtain additional editorial coverage will fall on deaf ears.

In the period just after the new-product introduction, it is always wise to follow up the press release fairly quickly with a case history news release describing how the new product is used in a particular application. This can often provide a second impact shortly after the first, one that will be as valuable as the advertising program that is likely to follow.

Another publicity technique commonly used is simple contact with key editors in the field. This might be done on a one-at-a-time basis or, under the right circumstances, in relatively small groups. The small-group approach is often valuable in the introduction of a new product that cannot support a full-blown press conference. Simply invite a few key editors to a luncheon and there describe the product informally.

Press relations should also be considered in conjunction with other new-product activities. For example, if a new product is to be introduced at an exhibit, special attention should be paid to the press to make sure that press representatives attend and that they see the right people. If a special demonstration becomes part of the new-product-introduction program, the press should be invited either to the main demonstration or to a preliminary one at the same location. Getting good press coverage for a new product is an extremely important aspect of new-product introduction, but it takes careful preparation and professional handling to get such coverage. We must keep in mind, however, that the editorial pages can also turn out to be a relatively unreliable medium.

Since there is a third party in the communications chain, the editor, one never knows exactly what is going to be said about the product, or how accurate the reporting will be. Nor is the amount of coverage that the press is likely to give the new product predictable. Because of these potential pitfalls, it is important that this segment of the introduction be in the hands of people who are knowledgeable and proficient in dealing with the press. It is important that all factual information be put in writing. Errors will invariably occur if this essential step is omitted. And it is important that editors be given *all* of the facts they are likely to encounter in the field. A professional newspaperman or business paper editor will consider any information he uncovers independent of the "official" source as exclusive information and will tend to inflate its importance in his printed story.

The press can be the biggest ally, or the biggest enemy, of a new-product introduction. It can also simply be neutral and ignore the subject. It is usually worthwhile to invest the time and money to help editors with the development of their stories—to the extent that they are written as accurately and as favorably as possible and so that the editors picture themselves as allies in the future development of the product. Though there are dangers involved in communicating to your audiences via the press, the advantages are so great that the potential problems and uncertainties should not deter a company from attempting this route. It is without question the route that reaches the largest number of people in the shortest amount of time. It is normally so much more efficient a medium for carrying new-product messages than other communications techniques that they should be deferred if necessary so as not to interfere with the coverage that the editors will provide for the new product.

SPACE ADVERTISING

Space advertising is probably the most commonly used and best understood segment of the marketing-communications field. It is so well known, in fact, that frequently the entire mass-communications area is referred to by the general term "advertising." Space advertising owes its prominence not only to its generally known and accepted effectiveness but to the fact that this area usually demands the largest number of dollars from the communications budget. Where, in publicity, the amount of space devoted to a product relates primarily to the strength of the product message and the skill with which that strength is presented to the editors, in advertising the amount of space devoted to the product is directly related to the amount of money invested in that space. Space advertising also differs from publicity in that the message is presented in exactly the way the comapny wants to present it instead of as edited and interpreted by a third party, the editor.

Because, in using space advertising, the company must invest funds for every bit of coverage it receives, it must always restrict placement of advertising to those areas where it is most likely to receive a satisfactory return for its investment. Where, in the publicity approach, it may be worthwhile to spend an hour or two in an attempt to get publicity in a publication where only a small segment of the audience is likely to be interested in the new development, the investment needed to carry any sort of message to the same audience by advertising would be too great to justify.

The basic investment that must be made in space advertising arises from two types of activities. The first is from the preparation of the advertising materials, the second from the purchase of media space. Since the bulk of the money normally goes into the purchase of the latter, the expenditures for advertising production become a relatively small consideration, normally running from 5 percent to 25 percent of the media cost. The budget for ad preparation is often given more consideration than it deserves, simply because it is a tangible area where people can see exactly what they are getting for their dollar. And they often follow a fixed rule on the ratio of production to space costs. But when we realize that the effectiveness of the fixed larger part of the expenditures, the space cost, can vary over a range of ten to one, because of quality and creative factors in the smaller part of the investment, we can come to no conclusion other than to look only at the total cost, and to do the best possible job in the initial preparation of the advertising materials, even if it involves a relatively higher cost for this segment.

When we look at all the possibilities for investment in media, it becomes apparent that this can become a bottomless well for advertising investment dollars. Almost any single field has 5 or 10 or 20 publications, and every field has 5 or 10 peripheral fields of interest, each of which has its own 5 or 10 or 20 publications. Add to this the many horizontal publications that serve each job function and the enormous cost potential becomes even more apparent.

Presumably, the allocation of funds to advertising must be made with some knowledge of what the media costs in that area are likely to be. But with that as a starting point, the next decision will call for allocation of media expenditures to provide the maximum in effectiveness from that advertising expenditure. Three interconnected areas of decision enter into this judgment. They are: (1) the selection of the media; (2) the frequency of placement in that media, and (3) the size of the ads.

At this point, the information needed to make these decisions has presumably been gathered and the marketing and advertising strategy been fixed. If you have a clear definition of the industries that should be reached and the job functions that are important, and the priorities of these audiences, the wealth of information available from the publications can guide you toward the most effective ones for the established objectives. This data is usually in the form of the audited circulation statements of the various publications, along with other pertinent information offered by the publishers. The Business Publications edition of Standard Rate and Data Service publishes much of this information on a monthly basis.

Circulation and other associated data that media professionals deem important are also gathered in a consistent format in the AIA Business Publication Data Form, a format established by and continually supervised by the Association of Industrial Advertisers, in cooperation with several other advertising and media-oriented organizations. Most important publications provide information in this format today, and the AIA approves it for conformity with the format, though not for accuracy of the content. The availability of this standard format from several different publications under consideration makes it far simpler to make objective comparisons than the use of the unformatted literature normally made available by the various publications. Further information on the AIA form, as well as an analysis of other factors in media selection, is contained in the book *Marketing and Media Evaluation,* edited by Robert Shiller, and prepared in conjunction with the same AIA committee that supervises the Media Data Form.

Despite all the available information, or perhaps because there is often too much of it, it is extremely difficult to select between the leading publications in some fields. Generally, where two publications serve approximately the same number of the same audience in the same way, and the advertiser's dollar limitations are such that he can use only one, it probably makes little difference which he chooses. Perhaps one will give him a slightly greater efficiency than the other, but in new-product introduction the game is won or lost by orders of magnitude, not by a few percentage points of efficiency.

Where one or two books do not dominate a field, so that a combination of magazines must be used to provide effective coverage, the problem of selection is more difficult. Data on overlap of readership is almost unavailable, and where it is available it is usually presented in a form heavily biased in favor of the publication that releases it. The categories of publication readers normally described on circulation statements are frequently not consistent with the audience as you define it in your product-introduction strategy. For example, if you have defined a segment of your desired audience as "upper level executives to whom the data processing function reports," you may find an analysis from the media that tells you how many "management" people are on the circulation lists of some publications, how many "financial management" people are on others, and even how many data processing management people are on a third. But unless someone has done a special study relating to your audience definition, you will be unable to get definitive information on the readership of any single publication by the group you are seeking—much less the duplication that may exist. Add to the list of problems the fact that publications normally report only their primary readership (subscribers or addressees), a figure that often represents only 20 to 30 percent of the total readers, and the magnitude of the problem of making optimum media decisions comes into focus. Because of these complexities, the problem of making the correct media decision is one that must be left to professionals who have worked their way through the mass of data available in the past, or to research that can clearly show who, defined in your terms, can be reached by which publications.

In a few areas, including the packaging industry and the business-government-financial community, data bases have been established that can give detailed readership and combination-readership data in forms adaptable to a wide variety of audience definitions—most of them consistent with the needs of most new products. But outside these areas, the research has to be done on an independent basis if the optimum selections are to be made.

The best way of doing such research is to develop a representative list of people who have been defined as the potential audience for the new-product message, and to survey them on their readership habits. To do this as an independent project, however, takes both time and money, so the efficiencies to be gained by better media selection must be sufficient to justify the cost. As a general rule, such research is justified if a program larger than $30,000 in space expenditures is contemplated, and consideration is being given to more than two publications.

Frequently, however, media readership can be determined as a tagalong question to a questionnaire designed to develop other information needed for strategy development at an earlier stage. In a recent introduction of a computer terminal, for example, a mail survey was conducted among people who were thought likely to have a potential interest in the product, to determine their level of experience in related technology areas. Though the information was designed to, and did, provide valuable inputs for marketing and sales direction, an additional question on publication readership provided the guidance needed to efficiently select media when the time came for introduction of the product.

Where either time or funding limitations prevent the use of research for developing media readership patterns among the target audiences, so that more traditional techniques of analyzing the data provided by the publications must be followed, professional advertising people in the company, or in an advertising agency, who have experience in making such evaluations, should be utilized in arriving at the media decisions. We must remember, however, that the unavailability of needed information and the complexity of the available information make these professional judgments rather than assuredly correct decisions. But because they are professional judgments, they are more likely to be right than if they had been made by those inexperienced in media selection. The project manager who substitutes his personal experience for such professional judgment does so at considerable risk.

The questions of amount of space and frequency of insertions are interrelated questions whenever dollar limits are imposed—as they normally are. The choice is between a smaller amount of space and greater frequency and a larger amount of space and less frequency. The question of course is which is the most productive approach.

Many factors go into this kind of decision. If development of inquiries is the sole objective, a two-thirds page to a one-page, black-and-white ad generally seems to be the most efficient space unit in terms of inquiries produced per dollar invested. But if the message is complex, it will take more space to get it across and greater frequency to develop the latent response. And if the nature of the product is such that company prestige must carry a certain part of the selling burden, the use of color or the use of double-page spreads or even larger space units must be considered. Larger space provides more impact and will normally produce greater reader retention.

Since the objective in most product communications is to get the message across as quickly as possible, large space units, such as double-page spreads, or four-, six-, or eight-page units to introduce a new product, are commonly and effectively used. Often these large introduction units are followed with smaller space units, such as one- or two-page colored ads that reflect the same basic graphics and thus remind people of the initial introduction advertising unit. The larger the ad and the greater the use of color, the more people will see the ad and the larger will be the number who will carry away the message. A smaller amount of space, while less costly, will be missed completely by a larger number of people. As in media selection, the decision between frequency and space size should be left to professionals who can balance the various factors and make judgments on the basis of their past experience.

Of course, the key to an effective advertising program is a creative approach and skillful execution. Book after book is filled with discussions of how to communicate through headlines and copy, the advantages and disadvantages of photographic techniques, art techniques, layout, use of two-color or three-color or four-color process techniques for getting reader attention, and various other tricks of the trade for getting reader action. The advertising professionals within both company and agency structures have generally spent many years in learning how to apply the few rules that exist and

how to balance the many factors that enter into such decisions. Rather than mislead the reader by providing an oversimplified summary of the body of knowledge, let me simply
suggest that the judgment of professionals be utilized and
relied upon in developing the most suitable advertising
approaches.

DIRECT MAIL

For carrying the message to its desired audience, direct
mail frequently plays a very important role in a new-product
introduction. The efficiency of direct mail is largely determined by the precision with which the potential buying influences for the new product can be identified. In a very real
sense, direct mail can be looked on as an extension of the
audience concentration offered by the trade publications. The
narrow, or "vertical," industry publications provide concentrated audiences with a single common denominator, but at a
higher cost per reader than the broad, or "horizontal," publications. If the audience that the prospective advertiser seeks is
concentrated within the readership of the smaller publication,
however, the higher cost per reader will be more than compensated for by the lower cost of the publication. Thus the
cost per targeted reader can be considerably lower in the
narrow, or "vertical," publication.

Direct mail is simply an extension of this concentration
principle, but it is concentrated in areas narrower than the
publications can serve. If the smallest publication in the target
field has a circulation of 20,000, but the product has only
1,000 potential users, it is often more economical to go to the
1,000 by mail than to the 20,000 through space—assuming of
course that the 1,000 can be identified.

The economic comparison between direct mail and space can be fairly complex. Where it costs between 2¢ and 5¢ per person to put a one-page publication advertisement in front of a reader, it can cost from 20¢ to 60¢ per person to put a relatively simple message in front of a person by mail. The differential narrows when we consider that the average simple direct-mail piece will be seen by approximately 60 percent of the intended audience, as compared to about 20 percent for the average space advertisement. By putting the numbers together it becomes obvious that at best direct mail costs twice as much per reader at an absolute minimum, and that where list development is difficult and print quantities are small, it can easily cost five to 20 times as much.

If we balance a tight direct mail list against a relatively small percentage of the audience of the publications serving the field who are, in truth, prospects for the new product, we can often come out with the conclusion that the economics favor direct mail. In the usual new-product situation, however, it is too oversimplified to break down an audience into those who are definitely prospects and those who are definitely not. We frequently see markets in which a relatively small number of people or companies are high-priority prospects and a much larger number are lower priority prospects, but good prospects nonetheless. For these situations it is often wise to run a space advertising program to reach the larger number, and combine it with a direct-mail program aimed at the more concentrated group of identified higher-priority prospects.

The economic comparison between space advertising and direct mail outlined above describes the comparative situation for a relatively simple message—a black-and-white advertisement versus a black-and-white direct-mail message. And economic analysis will show that the differences are small enough that it is often wise to use this kind of direct mail for prospecting among a relatively diluted audience, in much the same way that one prospects among an even more diluted audience via space advertising. But there is another kind of direct mail that falls outside the scope of simple dollar comparisons. This is the kind that uses the direct mail medium for its capability of enhancing the message, by taking advantage of creative approaches obtainable only through direct mail. Complex fold-out printed pieces are one example. Multipage brochures, tear-off reply cards that invite greater response than couponed ads, and dimensional objects that can help drive home the communications message are others. For these kinds of direct-mail programs, we can no longer think in terms of 15¢ and 20¢ per recipient, but often as much as 50¢ or $1 or $2 for elaborate printed items in fairly large quantity, and anywhere from $5 to $20 for dimensional objects mailed in boxes. The impact and memorability of these more elaborate mailings cannot be underrated. Where the new-product message is simple and clearly defined, it should be possible to get virtually 100 percent communication of the product message. And where inquiries are the objective, the higher rate of return that can be expected from reply cards enclosed in mailings, and the faster response that is possible, must also be considered significant factors by the product-introduction team.

No discussion on the use of direct-mail advertising is complete without a word on list development, for no direct mail is effective unless it reaches the right people. There are many sources of direct-mail lists ranging from lists available within companies, to those available from list rental houses, to those available from publications who maintain their lists in such a way as to permit sorting of various demographic groups from their general circulation lists. The Direct Mail

List edition of Standard Rate and Data Service is the best up-to-date directory of available lists, but even it is by no means complete. And despite the many subsegments of lists available from numerous sources, somehow the breakdowns never seem to coincide with the exact needs of the new-product-introduction strategy. If the direct-mail items are designed to be relatively simple printed pieces where the incremental cost of printing and mailing higher quantities is not too great, it is probably worthwhile to use whatever available lists come closest to the needs of the advertiser. Where more expensive mailing pieces are to be used or where the need for a long-range continuing mailing program is visualized, it may become worthwhile to build a list for the specific project.

Building a list can be a difficult procedure and can be so complicated and so different from situation to situation that if it is to be done for a reasonable cost and within reasonable time limits, the project had best be placed in the hands of professionals. The techniques may include buying an existing list and screening it against other sources to determine the identity of the most desirable prospects, or starting with a plant-census list broken down by the desired standard industrial classification numbers, and then using telephone techniques to identify by name the probable buying influences at those locations.

In the process of developing lists it is usually not too difficult to obtain the list of locations to which the product message should be sent. But tests of direct-mail effectiveness have shown quite clearly that mailings addressed to individuals are generally more effective than those addressed to company name only. Other tests, though, have indicated that mailings addressed to titles within company locations are often almost as effective as those addressed by name. The reason is probably that even the best lists addressed by individual name include a significant number of errors and obsolescence. These can be partially compensated for if the mailroom personnel redirect the mail to the right person. But unfortunately they might also redirect it out of the company to the person who has left. While the mailing by title may be partially ineffective because of the different meaning of the same title in different companies, carefully selected descriptive titles can often enable mailroom personnel to forward your item to the proper person. Therefore the possibility of mailing to titles, as a method of speeding up list development and obtaining reasonable efficiency, should not be overlooked. But even this course can present difficulties. If the direct-mail program involves a series of mailings to the same person, and should the company be large, the mailroom might conceivably designate a different recipient each time such a title mailing is received. Thus there is no guarantee that continuity can be achieved with title mailings.

PRODUCT LITERATURE

Product literature is so fundamental to any new-product-introduction communications program that this author is tempted to simply say "Yes, you need product literature," and let it go at that. Literature is needed to give the potential buyer a single source of all the information about the new product. Literature is needed by the salesman to leave with the prospect after he has made the call. Literature is needed as part of the inquiry-handling program to fulfill the promise of further information so often implied in the ads. Literature is often needed to suggest ideas to the buyer of how and where to use the product. New literature offers the opportunity for a second shot at publicity with a new-literature announcement following up the new-product announcement. And properly prepared literature can answer many of the questions about the use of the product that might otherwise require an extra call by a salesman, or even a technical-service call.

The question in a new-product-introduction program should never be a question of whether or not to produce literature—the only real question to be decided is that of scope. Should the literature be limited to a simple data sheet, a specification sheet, a how-to-use folder, or a full-color brochure loaded with application information? Perhaps what is needed is a literature series, each item oriented toward a different market. The decision as to what kind of literature is needed must be guided by the market factors discussed earlier and the strategy decisions behind the program.

Product-specification sheets normally represent the absolute minimum that should be considered. If difficulties are anticipated in buyer understanding of the proper use and potential limitations of the product, the literature must be extensive enough to cover these points. If there are multiple buying influences within the prospective buyer companies, some of whom will not have direct contact with the salesmen, then the literature must carry the sales story clearly and concisely to them. If the product is the kind that takes "faith" on the part of the purchasing customer in the ability of the product to do what is claimed for it, and faith in the capability of the supplier to back up its promises, then the literature must be of a quality consistent with the impression the company is trying to make. If the product is something like sophisticated computer gear that must be sold to the systems manager on the basis of how it works, as well as to someone else in the company on the basis of what it will do for him, then the literature has to carry both messages. Perhaps there should be two separate pieces of literature.

While the question of what kind of literature to produce is specific to each product and market situation, the question of how and when to get it produced is common to all new-product introductions. The preparation of any literature beyond the scope of the simple data or specifications sheet is a project in itself. And it is a project complicated by the fact that the information required for the literature is often not completely firm at the time it is needed. The minimum times needed for the various steps involved—writing, clearing, producing, and printing literature—are usually fairly long, and there is often enough recycling of the steps, because of changed conditions and requirements, to make the literature project take longer than is usually anticipated. As a result, the most frequent delay encountered in the early steps of new-product introductions is that in producing the new-product literature. But there are no simple solutions to the problem beyond careful planning, which must include both the timetabling of the steps involved and the coordination of those steps with the other product-introduction activities. Most important, the technical people and the product-management people involved in the new-product introduction must be made aware of the high priority that must be given the development of literature, usually at a time when other activities seem to demand equally high or higher priorities.

It happens frequently that the people who must provide the basic source information for the literature refuse to take the time, and only begin giving it priority when the lack of literature causes a sales bottleneck. Thus there arises a delay, often of several months' duration, before the literature is available. For most new-product introductions, the timetable must permit ample time for literature preparation, and the people who have to supply the information and review the copy must be made to recognize the significance of the project and the lead times needed for final production and printing.

EXHIBITS AND DEMONSTRATIONS

For certain types of products, such as machinery, control systems, or packaging materials, the most efficient way of communicating the potential contribution to a prospective buyer is to show it to him in action. This can best be done by demonstrating the new product in a booth at a trade show, or in a special showing of the product, or by putting a demonstration in a truck and moving it around the country, or by making a movie of the product in action, or by a variety of simulation techniques. The important common denominator of the demonstration technique is that the product is shown in action to a group of prospective buyers who have been invited either by the management of a trade exposition or the company involved.

The products that gain the most from this technique are those whose benefits can be readily seen, those that are too large or too heavy to be brought to a potential use site, and those whose mode of operation is difficult to explain. Such products include heavy machinery, auxiliary mechanical equipment, control systems, and materials destined to be used on mechanical equipment. While smaller items of machinery and other types of new products might also profit from exposure by demonstration, alternative techniques of showing them are normally available.

An industrial or trade exhibit, or exposition, as it is so often called, often provides an ideal place for demonstrating new products. If the product is too large to be moved, the basic contribution of the exhibit is to bring the prospective buyers to the product, instead of vice versa. Even if the product can logically be demonstrated at users' plants, the economics may favor investing in the exhibit space, where it can be shown to a large number of people at a lower cost than it would take to show it to them at their own plant locations.

If a new product is destined to serve a relatively narrow industry group, the introduction of it at an exhibit where a large percentage of the industry is represented would seem a highly logical communications strategy. Indeed, for many products it has proved to be a highly effective, low-cost technique for communicating the product capability to a large number of potential buyers in a very short time. However, the theoretical benefits of exhibit technique frequently cannot be taken advantage of. Most commitments for space must be made well in advance—for some shows as long as a year to a year and a half. Usually the timing decision for the new-product introduction cannot be made at the point in time when the commitment for exhibit space must be made. Of course, when the show is extremely important, and where it occurs only once in two or three or five years, the timing of the show might become a factor in the decision on timing for the new-product introduction. But this is the exception rather than the rule. Generally, other factors are more important in determining the timing of the introduction than the fact that an exhibit is available that can efficiently carry the product message. To hold back the product introduction for the show, or to push it forward before it is quite ready so that it can be demonstrated at the show, can lead to serious trouble.

Even if the timing does happen to work out, the introduction of a new product at a show does not always provide the great advantage that a company looks for. The very fact that many, many companies try to introduce their new products at the same show minimizes the attention that any one new product will get from both potential customers and the press—unless, of course, the product is the dominant one introduced at the show. If it is that, it will probably achieve great recognition. Where the product is something less than revolutionary, however, it is often more productive to introduce it two or three months before an exhibit, so that the publicity will appear before people go to the show. Thus prospective customers, having been alerted, will search out the booth at which the new product is to be demonstrated.

Whether the product is being introduced for the first time at the show, or demonstrated there shortly after its introduction, it is important that the demonstration be set up in such a way as to best communicate the product advantages to the potential buyer. A great amount of attention should be paid to designing the exhibit background, selecting floor space, and arranging the equipment demonstrations in such a way that the communication strategy is clearly transmitted. The approach will vary, of course, from product to product, and the detailed approach should be the province of exhibit experts. Similarly, the design of the exhibit and the complex logistical planning required for a satisfactory demonstration at a trade show must all be in the hands of people with relevant experience. And budget planning must take into account the many "extra" costs that are incurred in exhibits.

The use of the demonstration technique does not end with trade expositions, however. The really innovative uses of demonstrations and related techniques are most often to be seen when a demonstration of the product is a key element in the marketing-introduction strategy. If the item is small and portable, no real problem exists beyond providing the salesmen with demonstration models and demonstration instructions. Where a complex piece of equipment is involved, however, or where the demonstration of auxiliary equipment or materials must be made on a piece of major equipment, the use of demonstrations as a market-communications tool is another matter.

One technique has been to establish demonstration locations either at plants where the equipment is installed on a test basis, or at other locations selected for the occasion, and then arrange demonstrations for prospective buyers. If such a strategy is to be used, advertising and direct mail also must be used to get the proper attendance. A well-planned demonstration given to less than a capacity audience is a waste of company resources. Often the real creativity must go into approaches for attracting prospective buyers to the demonstration.

Such demonstrations are, of course, major planning and logistical problems in themselves. Locations must be developed, the equipment must be moved to the right place, supporting utilities must be available, labor contracts must be adhered to, local regulations must be observed, entertainment facilities must often be provided, lists of prospective buyers must be obtained, and a program must be established for bringing people to the demonstration and then following up afterward. While a great deal of manpower is involved in setting up such demonstrations, a lot of this is not necessarily salesman manpower. This is an especially important consideration in a situation where a new sales force must be established to support the new product. In such circumstances, only a relatively small number of trained salesmen are likely to be available in the early stages of the introduction.

Sometimes, to avoid the problems of setting up the demonstration at a series of locations, it is more economical to bring key buyers to a single location where the demonstration is to be held. Since this involves arranging for, and probably paying for, long-distance transportation, it is usually a practical approach only for a high-priced item that is destined to be sold to a very small number of buyers.

Another technique is to set up a truck trailer as a portable demonstration unit, and arrange a series of local demonstrations. This reduces logistical problems—the demonstration has to be set up only once—but there is still the problem of attracting audiences. It is a very good approach, of course, for the kind of product that has fairly broad appeal and can thus be shown in a large number of cities. Yet before attempting such a course, you should pay careful attention to cost-estimating, for this approach often calls for the full-time services of truck drivers and technicians as well as expensive equipment, rented or purchased, and the costs are likely to run considerably higher than one might expect.

A compromise technique frequently used is a motion picture, which can show the action of a machine in a way a printed description cannot. While the motion picture is ordinarily not as effective a communications tool as the live demonstration, it can often handle a very large part of the job. Indeed, with some items, certain motion-picture techniques—such as animation and slow motion—can perhaps do a better job than live demonstration. Thus the decision will depend on the product.

As with all demonstration techniques, caution is the word here. The production of a film is usually very expensive and more time-consuming than most people estimate. Special techniques that clarify the explanation also raise the cost tremendously. A project manager will often think: "Why not simply take some movies of the machine in operation and use that? How expensive can that be?" Yet when he sees the results, he is usually dissatisfied, and he demands a more sophisticated production. As a result, the costs rise far beyond the original estimates. The public today—and the public includes both the project manager and the industrial buyer—has become accustomed to watching highly sophisticated films. Any film that does not include something at least approaching sophistication creates an image of cheapness or shabbiness for the project it is designed to support. Thus the image created by the film itself can do more harm than the message does good.

But if a more sophisticated film is produced, and its higher cost supported, how long will it be useful? We all know that most new products do not retain their original configurations very long, since changes are made after the product is introduced and reaction is developed from the marketplace. We know, too, that the selling points often anticipated as being the strongest turn out weak, and new selling points take their place as marketing experience is gained. Thus an expensive film, made to introduce a new product, might become totally obsolete in six months or a year. And the problem of getting people to the movie, or the movie to the people, can be as great, or greater, than getting them to a live demonstration. So these costs must be borne too. For these reasons the movie is usually not the low-priced substitute for a demonstration that most people think it is.

This is not to say that the motion picture has no place in new-product introduction. It and all other alternatives should be looked at. But they should be looked at critically and objectively and with a full appreciation of the cost of doing the job properly.

OTHER COMMUNICATIONS TECHNIQUES

There are a variety of communications techniques in common use by consumer advertisers that are commonly ignored by industrially oriented marketing communications people. These include radio, television, billboards, car cards, skywriting, matchbook advertising, and so on. While these rarely find a place in the introduction of a new industrial product, they should not be ignored completely. They are well-established vehicles of communication that do play an occasional role in an industrial new-product introduction.

Any of these techniques can be used to support attendance at a trade exposition, especially if the show is in a relatively small community. In the popular convention mecca of Atlantic City, a billboard or an airplane streamer that says "See the new gadget at Booth 525" may be an effective way of getting more people to that demonstration in which your company has invested so much money. And matchbooks distributed at a hotel that serves as headquarters for the group containing the largest number of potential buyers of your new product might be an effective way of beginning to communicate with them.

While these represent rather individualized, special-situation opportunities, the often overlooked consumer technique of radio advertising, and to some extent newspapers, has a broader application in new-product introduction. Many industries are concentrated in relatively small geographic areas. The automotive industry is concentrated in Detroit, the rubber industry in Akron and New England, computers in Poughkeepsie, Philadelphia, and Boston, electronics in the bay area near San Francisco, the oil industry on the Gulf Coast and the West Coast. A new product that serves one of these, or a similar concentrated industry, can effectively utilize local newspapers, or radio spots, or even television, for the introduction of certain types of products.

One key advantage of radio is speed. If the objective of the communications program is to develop inquiries, the development and placement of ads in monthly trade publications, followed by the lag time usually encountered in receiving inquiries, can easily run to three to four months. With radio, the ads can be written in less than a week and placed in days, and inquiries can be received on the same day that the commercials run—through a special telephone number.

The local nature of spot radio can be an advantage as well as a disadvantage, depending on the introduction strategy. If a product has to be heavily supported by technical service, it is usually a mistake to make a broad product offering across the country before service is made available in all locations. The product can be introduced by radio and newspapers at one location at a time, as the technical service facilities for each area are established.

Another area where radio might prove efficient is where the product is sold to a wide variety of industries. Items such as hand tools, office equipment, or commercial services fall into this classification. The concentration of potential buyers of such products may be as great on radio as in any other communications medium, so radio might prove to be a medium not only for the introduction communications, but for long-range promotion of the product. One successful example was the introduction of a new data-service center in New York City. Since it was a purely local service that could not be economically promoted in publications with broad geographic distribution, local media were used. Of them all, and they included newspapers and direct mail, radio stood out as the prime source of traceable business for the new operation—and at a cost per dollar of sale many times lower than that of the next medium.

5

Communicating
Via the Salesmen

The most effective of the various communications vehicles available for use in introducing a new product is the salesman who carries the product-information story directly to the potential buyer. Unlike the mass-communications vehicles described in previous chapters, the salesman can seek out the proper recipient for the sales message and then tailor the sales presentation to his specific needs. He can even go beyond that and identify and solve specific problems that stand in the way of converting buyer interest into a positive sale.

But this effectiveness is purchased at an extremely high cost—in time, in traveling expenses, in wasted effort in seeing the wrong people, and in wasted time waiting to see the right people. The inefficiencies are so great that the current average cost of an average single industrial sales call is estimated by McGraw-Hill's research department at more than $50. This high cost, coupled with the limitation in the number of calls that any sales force can make within a fixed time span, leads most marketers to optimize sales costs by using some mix of direct sales and mass communications. Several sophisticated studies in the recent past have clearly shown that selling costs for mature products are considerably reduced by a proper mix of mass communications and direct sales expenditures. There is every reason to believe that this is also true for new products. And the fact that new products have a finite time frame within which the selling job must be done points to an even greater need for emphasizing mass communications.

But whatever the mix of investment between mass communications and direct sales, it is also extremely important that the communications ability of the salesmen be increased to the maximum, so that they can produce the greatest possible results for their cost. To operate at maximum efficiency, salesmen must be familiar with the product, with its advantages and disadvantages, and with market needs. They must be guided in seeking out the plant locations that represent the maximum potential, and the people within those locations who are the most likely buying influences. And they must be provided with the kind of materials that can help them more efficiently communicate the new-product message. Put another way, the entire communications strategy will do only half its job if it is merely translated into an effective mass-communications program. It must also be communicated effectively to the salesmen so that they can take advantage of the information inputs and the market-priority strategies that the mass-communications program is built on.

In developing a communications program for the salesmen, the choice of effective techniques varies with the sales organization. The salesman for the new product, the individual who carries the product message directly to the potential user, may be a direct salesman who is part of the company, or he may be a distributor, a manufacturer's representative, or a salesman in such an organization. The latter group may require special attention if they are to take full advantage of the information offered.

Two kinds of techniques are commonly used for communicating with the salespeople—person-to-person contact and the printed page. Other techniques, such as closed-circuit television, movies, and similar substitutes for personal contact, are less frequently considered, because they are generally too expensive or too time-consuming in their development to be truly applicable to the introduction situation.

SALES MEETINGS

The most common method for providing sufficient information to the salesman to enable him to comfortably handle face-to-face new-product selling situations is to use the same face-to-face technique where he can develop in-depth knowledge of the new product and market in an atmosphere where he can get his own questions answered. This is normally accomplished at a sales meeting. The product is usually described in detail and the salesmen are educated on the probable environment within which the new product is to be utilized. They are informed of the sales policies, the sales objections, the nature of the competition, and all the other things they might come up against in trying to sell the new product. Time should normally be left for considerable discussion, for if the salesman goes away from the meeting with some of his questions unanswered, he will not feel comfortable about having such questions arise when he is face-to-face with the customer.

Thus the sales meeting should be very carefully planned as an educational experience, and any and all types of educational techniques should be used. Demonstrations, flip charts, slides, role-playing, and so on, should be brought into the sales-meeting program, not only to help communicate to the salesmen, but to probe the degree to which the communications are getting through and being accepted. When the salesman leaves the sales meeting, he should feel he has all the answers he needs. If he does not feel that way, it is usually because the meeting was not properly planned and executed. And if he does not feel that he has all the answers, he will not easily and comfortably plunge himself into a possibly embarrassing sales situation and this reluctance will show up later in the sales figures.

The sales meeting is not necessarily a single unit. It might take the form of a series of regional meetings, or a series of distributor meetings too.

SALES MANUALS

We all know that in a school situation, lectures are normally combined with textbooks. Similarly, salesmen should not leave a new-product-introduction sales meeting without printed material in their hands. Not everything that is said at the sales meeting will be remembered later on, so it is important that all significant information be made available to the salesmen in an easy-to-get-at reference document in which they can easily find the answers to the questions likely to arise. A common technique for satisfying this requirement is to prepare and distribute a sales manual. This can include such sections as technical description, possible application areas, case histories of use, market descriptions, lists of potential buyers, sales policies, prices and terms, promotional program description, and available sales aids and references.

Sales manuals should be so organized that additions can be made as new information is developed, for there will always be such additions and changes in the early phase of new-product experience. One technique is to use a loose-leaf format and a letter-and-page-number system for each section that permits the insertion of new pages in the proper sequence. Thus, when new information is developed, it can be sent to the salesmen, properly coded to fit into the logical section of the sales manual.

The key to sales-manual development lies in the expected-use pattern. If a salesman is in a prospect's office and is asked a detailed question, he should be able to turn quickly to the right section and find the answer almost immediately. If he must rummage through the book to find the answer, his alternate course of action will be to tell the customer that he does not have the answer, and then either search through the book later when he has more time, or call headquarters for the information. Thus he is forced to take the time to make another call on the potential customer to get to a stage in communications that could have been resolved during the earlier call. So the indexing and organization of the manual, and the ease with which information can be retrieved from it, are extremely important.

As further information is developed during the early part of the product introduction, continuing communications with all salesmen must be maintained. This can be through letters describing any items of interest to the salesmen, or it can be in the form of additional sheets to be included in the sales manual. Often a combination is desirable.

One of the best techniques for improving sales efficiency is to make sure that the salesmen gain from the experiences of the others. Introducing a new product is like exploring virgin territory, where nobody quite knows what he will run into. It can therefore be of extreme value to each salesman to learn what kinds of obstacles his associates are running into, and to learn where and how they have achieved their successes. One technique for communicating such information is for the central headquarters group to provide a clearing-house service. From incoming salesmen call reports, pertinent material for mailing to all the other salesmen can be selected. Another convenient technique is to establish a standard case-history reporting form. The details of every new installation can be reported in detail to the other salesmen. Segments of such a form might call for such information as location of the installation, type of business served, specific needs of the buyer that led to the sale, cost comparison with previous system, time of installation, and attitude of the buyer toward showing it to others. Each specific product would call for its own specific information.

Not many people do it, but it is just as important to record case histories of lost sales. If a program operating at the early stages of product information can communicate the case history of sales that are not made as well as those that are, the salesmen will be able to avoid their colleagues' mistakes and function more efficiently.

Other techniques available for sales communications include letters, frequent visits by sales management and technical people, and even a steady stream of cassette recordings. All of these require the commitment of significant time by marketing management. But all such techniques can help keep the salesmen up to date in the early stages of new-product introduction when information is usually transient.

OTHER SALES AIDS

Another significant way of communicating is to provide the salesmen with presentation materials to help them better organize and tell their stories. Sales aids cover a variety of techniques that can range from simple literature to flip charts, slide films, movies, demonstration materials, and models of the equipment.

Literature is perhaps the most common sales aid. Usually a great deal of thought has gone into its organization, with the intention of making it the most effective and complete presentation of the new-product information possible. The salesmen often find, with or without formal guidance, that the organization of the sales literature works well for them, too, in presenting the product story to prospective buyers. Often they find that the best initial sales-presentation technique is to go through the literature page by page, amplifying the points made as they see the need for such amplification. Thus the sales presentation is orderly and complete, and the piece of literature can be left behind as a reminder of the points made, as well as for use inside the buyer organization by people other than those who heard the presentation.

The flip charts can become an extension of the brochure. A flip chart is usually designed in such a way that the points are made one at a time in proper order. Photographs and diagrammatic or graphic material that can help to clarify certain points are presented on the flip charts, while the order of presentation and a few key words act as cues. Frequently, in new-product introductions, the flip chart and brochure are planned together so as to utilize the same art elements and the same basic organization of presentation.

Often the salesmen are provided with a set of slides. Though this creates an equipment problem, it has an advantage over the flip charts in that it can be shown to a larger group of people. The salesmen can modify the order of the presentation too, and customize the same basic presentation material to the individual needs of different buying industries.

Slide films are an extension of the flip chart and slide

presentation, with the significant difference that the organization of the slide film must be followed exactly, and that the words are provided by the narrator of the slide film with no opportunity for adaptation to the individual situation. Slide films are particularly useful where the salesmen are not yet fully trained, so that the "fixed" presentation will be more effective than the average salesman's presentation. They are also useful in situations where it is felt that it would be best to tell the whole story without interruption, before handling interruptions, objections, or other discussion by the prospective buyers.

Movies, of course, do everything the slide film does, with additional opportunities for showing mechanical operation or a new principle via animation, and showing the actual equipment or material flowing through a process. Movies come the closest of all the sales-aids techniques to mixing the sales presentation with the actual demonstration of the new product.

Demonstration units are another type of sales aid, useful for certain situations. Where the product is small and portable, the demonstration might include the actual product. Or if the new product is based on a key technological difference, the difference might be displayed in some kind of a two-dimensional or three-dimensional working model. In the right situation, such working models can greatly help the salesmen to communicate the properties, the advantages, and the differences involved in the new product.

The real difficulty with all of these formalized communications aids is the salesmen's resistance to their use. In so many cases where professional communications people at the headquarters level feel that such aids are necessary to help the salesmen communicate, the salesmen feel that they only get in the way. Their basis for this feeling is that their relationship with the people to whom the sales message is directed becomes strained by the formal nature of the communications aid. They feel they can develop far greater rapport in selling based on informal conversation. While this may be true, and certainly is true for some of the top salesmen who can communicate fully through informal techniques, the choice for most salesmen is between organized communications and fancied rapport. While the rapport is of prime importance in a continuing selling activity, communications generally plays a more important role in the introduction of new products. That salesmen feel that the formalized presentation will reduce rapport is usually more an indication of their own discomfort with the presentation than the fear that the customer will see it as an interference with normal communications.

With such problems standing in the way of the use of formalized sales aids, many companies decide not to use them at all. Others prepare them and the salesmen fail to use them. In only a relatively few situations are they properly prepared and used by the salesmen to their fullest extent. If we look closely at the companies that utilize them properly and those that do not, we see two fundamental areas of difference. The first lies in how they go about developing the sales presentation, the second in how it is presented to the salesmen.

The successful development of a sales presentation calls for a period of testing and piloting to make the presentation work best in the situation between the salesman and the potential customer. Almost no preparer of presentation materials, whatever his qualifications and experience, has enough foresight to hit on the optimum organization sequence and tone for the presentation from the sterile position of non-contact with the potential customers. To really make the presentation work, someone must take it to potential customers and try it out. Invariably some modifications, to improve the flow and minimize the interference with rapport, will have to be made after this piloting phase.

The second step, which is so often missed, especially with the formal types of presentations in which the salesmen have to participate, is to see that the salesmen get experience in working with the presentation. If they are unfamiliar with it, there is no question but that they will hesitate to use it with important prospects—and they might never pass the point where they feel comfortable enough with it to subject any prospect to it. If, during the sales training phase, we can get the salesmen to familiarize themselves with using the presentation to the point where they are in fact comfortable with it, they will use it far more often and with far greater effectiveness in their normal sales contacts.

One of the best ways of doing this is to spend considerable time on the use of the sales aids at the initial sales meeting where the salesmen receive their product indoctrination. The use of the sales aid must be carefully explained and demonstrated, and the salesmen must then use it under the controlled conditions of a sales simulation. Usually this is accomplished by splitting up the salesmen into working groups, and having each salesman demonstrate the product to group members. Plenty of time must be allowed during this training session for comments, criticism, and discussion of the use of the sales presentation. If the procedure can be repeated again after a day or a week, the salesmen will become even more familiar and more comfortable in the use of the sales aid, and it will then serve them and the company effectively.

There are other procedures by which these principles of familiarizing salesmen with the sales aids, and making them comfortable in using them, can be gotten across. But unless considerable time is spent on this activity, chances are that the sales aids will be used very little. The company that spends $5,000 to $10,000 in the preparation of a flip chart or set of slides and then mails it to the salesmen can expect little for its investment and would be better advised to invest elsewhere. The company that adds an investment in training to the investment in original development will probably get a very satisfactory return.

The cost of preparing sales-aids materials is commonly considered part of the "advertising," or mass communications, budget rather than part of the direct sales budget. This accounting practice, however, often leads to erroneous decisions as to the acceptable budget level for sales-aid material. An advertising manager, in allocating his budget, will typically look at the alternative uses for the $5,000 to $30,000 expenditure that might be involved in sales-aid development, and compare its effectiveness with the thousands of people that he can reach for the same amount. As he looks at the small number of salesmen that would use the aid, and the number of customers they can reach with it, he will often conclude that the number is too small to justify such an expensive and time-consuming project.

On the other hand, if the project is looked at as a sales function and evaluated in terms of the increased efficiency on the part of the salesmen that it can provide, a totally different conclusion may be reached. Even if only one or two salesmen are on the staff, but the nature of the product is such that their effectiveness can be doubled by the use of some kind of sales aid, there is justification for spending funds on the sales aid equivalent to the salesmen's salary and overhead expenses. While many marketing people will automatically discount development of sales-aid materials for a small sales force, they must recognize that a potential increase of sales efficiency is as important a factor in the decision relating to the use of sales aids as the number of salesmen, and it is often very sound economics to develop sophisticated sales tools even for a very limited sales force.

6

Sequencing
the Product Launch

As was pointed out earlier, a large number of activities are normally involved in the introduction of a new industrial product. Most of these are communications-oriented activities, since communications is really what the launching process is all about. The tools commonly used include space advertising, publicity, direct mail, merchandising materials, literature, samples, exhibits, special events, internal communications, sales training, and inquiry handling and follow-up. In any new-product introduction, some mix of two or more of these elements is normal. In order to obtain the maximum effectiveness, from each communications technique, the sequence in which they are used must be carefully planned. Each new-product situation has its own particular product and market characteristics, its own competitive situation, its own degree of newness and degree of differentiation from other products, its own resource factors, and, because of these individual characteristics, its own market-penetration strategy. And the sequence of the product introduction will therefore vary from situation to situation.

Certain general rules apply to most introductions. It is axiomatic that sales training must be completed before the public introduction. It is also obvious that the publicity coverage will be minimized if ads appear before the publicity articles are written, for editors are not prone to consider material already exposed in advertising as top quality news. So, unless there is a compelling reason to do otherwise, publicity must precede space advertising.

Literature, of course, should always be available—if not before the formal introduction, at least within a few days afterward. Otherwise, there is unlikely to be a satisfactory follow-up to the interest that has been generated. The same is true of inquiry follow-up and handling techniques, which must be in place shortly after inquiries are received.

Exhibits are extremely important for certain types of products, especially heavy machinery and similar products, which must be seen in operation to be fully appreciated. For these the exhibit may be the key step in the timing and sequencing of the introduction program. In certain industries exhibits take place very infrequently—sometimes as seldom as once in five years. If the new product fits into that type of industry, and exhibits are important to the nature of the product, the dominating factor in the sequencing of the new-product introduction would undoubtedly be the exhibit. Technical meetings, too, are often the logical place for introducing a new product, and if so, the timing should be adjusted accordingly.

For a typical new-product introduction when the product has a relatively wide potential usage among audiences not too clearly defined, the optimum sequence would probably be something like the following:

1. Sales training
2. Press conference
3. Literature
4. Inquiry handling
5. Space advertising

Such an introduction follows the traditional pattern of introduction via a press conference (or news release), with literature and inquiry handling available shortly thereafter, followed by a space advertising program. For a product that has a very clearly defined market and a potential competitor breathing down its neck, the sequence might be completely reversed:

1. Sales presentation
2. Literature
3. Sales training
4. Direct mail
5. Publicity
6. Inquiry handling

Here the initial introduction is made by direct mail and organized sales contact, complemented by a sales presentation so that potential customers can be fully informed of the product and its characteristics before the competitors have a clear picture of your activity. Often advertising and publicity in a situation like this are used for prestige and reminder value, and for communicating to secondary buying influences, rather than to carry the message to primary customers, all of whom will have been contacted before the public announcement.

For a new product such as a very large piece of machinery, it is often desirable to make the formal introduction at a press conference several months before a major exhibit as indicated in this sequence:

1. Publicity
2. Space advertising
3. Literature
4. Sales training
5. Exhibit
6. Inquiry handling

With this sequence, a potential customer can be informed of the product and will know to look for it at the exhibition. On the other hand, if it is felt that it is necessary to demonstrate the product to the press in order to maximize press interest, and if it is a difficult type of product to assemble for a press showing, it might prove most economical, with minimum loss of effectiveness, to arrange a press introduction at the time of the exhibit when the product is already set up, and to arrange a sales training session in the days immediately preceding the exhibit. There are a large number of possible combinations of introduction sequences. If a product's technical capabilities are still uncertain, the salesmen may be given the first opportunity to show it. This will make it possible to avoid massive criticism should the product have to go back to the drawing boards. If the product is so broad in its applications that the salesmen have no hope of pinpointing key target accounts, the sales training and presentation steps can await the development of inquiries, whose analysis can then serve as a guide to sales follow-up.

But whatever the decision in sequencing the various steps of the new-product introduction, the real problem arises in completing the various elements of the project within a reasonable time span. Rarely is there enough time available to do the kind of job on the communications elements that the professionals would tell you they need. One common reason is that, after having gathered the necessary information and having made the decision to launch the product, management rarely feels that an additional delay is warranted, even if the resultant rush means compromises in communications quality.

Complicating the job of timing and sequencing is the problem of preparation times, which differ greatly from communications technique to communications technique. Literature, especially highly technical literature, usually has an extremely long preparation time. Similarly, the placing of advertisements in a trade publication may have a reasonably long lead time, largely because the closing dates for placement are often a month ahead of the distribution data. Direct mail may vary in its lead time from days to months depending on the availability of the lists and the complexity of the direct-mail piece.

Sales training can be handled in as little as one day or as much as several months depending on the complexity of the product. Advertisements take from a week to three months for preparation, depending on clearance times, use of color, and the like. A news release might be prepared and released in a matter of days. But a press conference, especially one whose purpose is to introduce a new product, can rarely be put on without two to six weeks of preparation. It is obvious that the lead time for each element must be taken into consideration in making the sequencing decisions and in meeting the timetable. It is to the techniques of timetabling that we turn next.

USING PERT FOR NEW-PRODUCT INTRODUCTION

The timing sequence of a complex new-product introduction is difficult to plan by normal timetabling techniques, largely because of the interdependence of the various elements. For such programs, one method that has proved effective is the use of one of the various "network analysis" techniques, generally referred to as "critical path" or "PERT" techniques. While the two terms have some difference in meaning for highly sophisticated practitioners, they both involve planning and sequencing the detailed elements of a complex program in terms of the various steps that have to be accomplished.

What Is PERT?

The letters P-E-R-T once stood for Program Evaluation and Review Technique. Today its applications have gone so far beyond evaluation and review that the term PERT is used more as a coined word than as a set of initials. First developed as a system for managing the complex interrelated development efforts involved in the Polaris program, PERT is credited with cutting as much as two years off the scheduled time for this project. Since then it has become a generally accepted technique in both government and industry for planning and controlling complex development and construction projects. While there are some technical differences between "critical path," "PERT-Time" and "PERT-Cost" systems, the term PERT is used here to cover all the variations.

The PERT system involves diagraming the various steps that make up a project as a series of consecutive, parallel and interconnected paths. It establishes a rigid pattern for diagraming the steps in a program, with boxes representing definable points in time, or "events," and lines representing the "activities" involved in accomplishing these steps. PERT has the advantage over other timetable techniques in that it recognizes the fact that certain elements of a program can be accomplished concurrently, while other elements must be done consecutively. When a program is complex, these interrelationships cannot always be kept clear. . . .

The basic elements of a critical-path diagram can be shown from the accompanying, oversimplified example.

Reproduced by permission of *Industrial Marketing*.

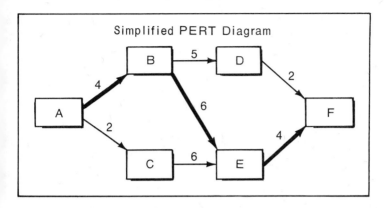

The diagram says that the activities leading to events B and C can begin only when A is complete. D can begin when B is complete but E cannot begin until both B and C are complete. The project can be completed (F) only after D and E are complete. The estimated times needed to complete each step are indicated and it is obvious that the critical path, or the series of steps which determines the time limits for completion of the project, is A-B-E-F, which would take 14 time units. The reason for determining it can be simply to schedule the project, or to shorten it. Time savings in activity A-B, B-E, or E-F can shorten the project time, while savings in A-C, C-E, B-D, or D-F will have no effect. Sometimes overall time can be shortened by taking attention away from the less critical areas and turning it toward the more critical ones.

In a large project, once the steps are determined, the various events and sequences can be fed into a computer. Progress on completion of the individual events can be fed in, and the computer can generate periodic reports that indicate what segments are falling behind schedule. Thus corrections can be made long before the delay shows itself in failure to meet the final deadline. Computerized networks are being used every day in major construction jobs and in many development programs, especially those serving the Department of Defense and the National Aeronautics & Space Administration.

These more refined techniques are hardly applicable to the relatively simple jobs with which the communications area is concerned. In these, the major contribution of the PERT technique is in providing a disciplined pattern for planning and follow-up.

A PERT diagram consists of a group of blocks, each representing a specific and identifiable point in the progress of a project. The blocks are arranged on paper with connecting arrows indicating which events come before and which come after each step. This provides a clear picture that shows what parts of the job can proceed concurrently and what parts must be accomplished in sequence. From such a diagram, the manager can easily determine the shortest possible time in which the entire job can be done and where the potential bottlenecks lie. (See the description of PERT on page 148.)

The following is an example of how the network analysis technique actually was used in a new-product situation.

The new product was a new family of ethylene vinyl acetate copolymers, a series of plastics with many of the performance properties of rubber.

The decision to go ahead was made in January. The material had been in market-development stage for over a year, and several customers had developed uses for it which were close to commercialization.

We also knew that at least two other companies were well along in ethylene vinyl acetate copolymer technology. Though we felt we had something of a lead, we could not be sure how long it would be before they, too, would be ready for commercial introduction.

One part of the audience was clearly defined as plastics and rubber processors. A second part was less clearly defined as industrial designers and other people with materials responsibilities in a wide variety of user industries. The company already had salesmen calling on the plastics processor part of this group. But we'd had no previous contact with rubber processors or with the wide variety of end-users to whom this product would be of interest. It was clear that we would have to use a number of mass-communications techniques, and use them quickly and efficiently, if we were to get our message to all these people before our competitors could catch up and introduce a similar product.

The first determination was the desired sequence for completion of each element in the program as shown in Figure 6.

The key to the timetable became the date of the press conference, which was dictated by the closing dates of some of the major publications involved. This press conference date was fixed as March 10.

We recognized that the information had to be presented to our salesmen before this date, and the presentation to salesmen would have to include both the news release and the literature. This fixed the date at which the literature and release had to be completed. The press conference date also fixed the time by which the physical arrangements for the press conference had to be completed. This included such things as developing the list of invitees and making arrangements for catering of refreshments.

Since many of the magazines serving this particular market are monthlies, we knew it would be at least one month before the publicity articles resulting from the press conference would be published. Knowing that the publications prefer not to have an announcement ad appear in the same issue as their news articles, this fixed the earliest date for appearance of the ad at some 45 working days after the press conference.

Since we were under no such restrictions with direct mail, we scheduled the first of several mailers for the day after the press conference. Again, knowing this would bring in inquiries we had to have our complete inquiry-handling system in operation about three days after the direct mail piece was sent out.

Figure 6. Desired end results of product-introduction program are shown in the black boxes. This is final part of total PERT diagram.

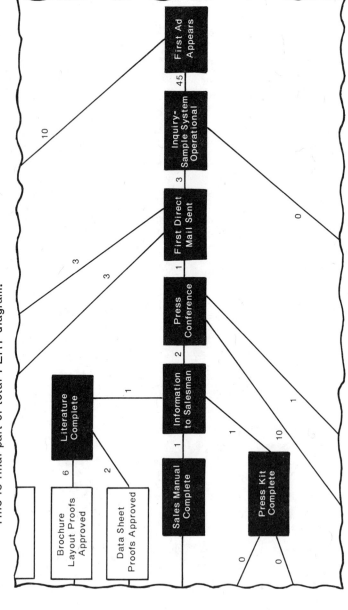

The next big problem was preparation of the many elements of the program according to the timetable. The key elements are shown in black in Figure 7.

Certain activities had to be completed before other elements of the program could get under way. For example, basic technical information on the product had to be received before we could prepare literature, the salesmen's manual or the news release. We needed case histories for the news release and the salesmen's information book and, possibly, for the ad program and the direct mail. Activities such as publicity and preparation of data sheets could proceed without specific budget authorization, but procedures called for budget approval before we could undertake the more expensive space advertising and direct mail programs, and preparation of a major piece of literature.

Once the time limitations at the end of the program were established and the starting points established at the beginning, it was relatively easy to list the key activities in the preparation of each of the programs. For example, for a space program, the key steps are:

> Ad program proposal complete
> Budget submitted
> Budget approved
> Ad program approved
> Ad copy-layout complete
> Ad copy-layout approved
> Ad mechanicals complete
> Ad mechanicals approved
> Ad electros to publication
> Ad appears

Similar steps are involved in every other segment of the communications program.

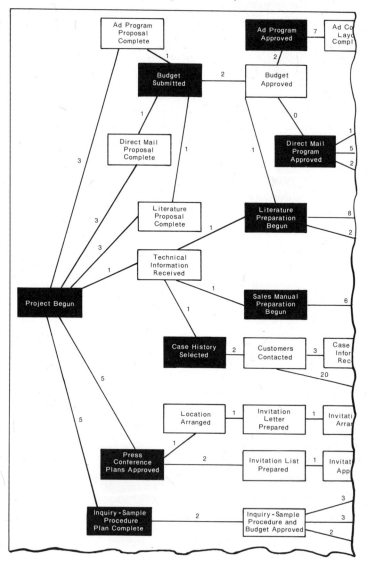

Figure 7. Elements in black boxes had to be completed before other parts of program could proceed.

To avoid complicating the diagram too greatly we limited the events listed to the more critical ones, knowing full well that there are many other steps which must be undertaken in the ordinary course of preparing advertising material. We also decided to diagram only the first direct-mail piece to avoid complicating the diagram.

All of the events and their preceding and succeeding events reduced to a single diagram resulted in a rather complex-looking Figure 8. Following established critical-path technique, each block represents a clearly defined event and each connecting line represents an activity. The numbers on the lines represent the number of working days estimated to be needed for that particular activity.

When the entire diagram was pulled together, the next step was to identify the critical path, which is another way of saying the series of steps that takes the longest time.

It was apparent in this situation that there were two critical paths. These are shown in the heavy lines. One critical path involved preparation of the brochure. The other involved preparation of the direct-mail piece. As a matter of fact it was apparent that there weren't enough days available to complete either program. Another potential problem existed in getting the case-history information, which involved contact with those customers who had started to use the product during the market-development phase.

By calling attention to these time limitations, the diagram made its greatest contribution. We simply gave the brochure and case-history items highest priority, pushed them hard in the early stages and completed them in less time than our original estimate. We couldn't rush preparation of the direct-mail piece, since it involved an outside supplier molding samples of the product, so we substituted a news release with

Figure 8. Heavy black lines indicate the two critical paths — the series of steps requiring the most time — in this new-product-introduction program.

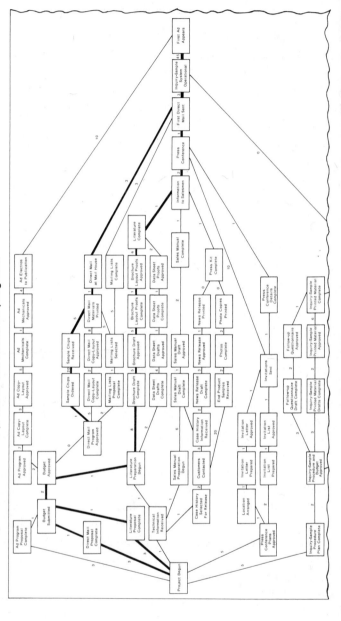

a note attached, and sent the originally planned direct-mail piece several weeks later.

It is especially interesting to note that preparation of the ad, the project usually thought of first in a situation like this, could be delayed until after the other elements were completed. This knowledge permitted us to turn maximum attention to preparation of the other materials.

The diagram clarified something else. Though we needed the salesmen's manual and the literature at the same time, the literature had a much longer production time. Thus, a technical writer was able to finish writing the literature, then turn his attention to the sales manual while the literature was being produced.

We anticipated that follow-up of all the inquiries would strain the capabilities of our field sales force. We therefore arranged to have a service organization with a nationwide network of technically trained telephone interviewers screen all inquiries, so that only active prospects would be called to the salesman's attention.

We also anticipated difficulties in filling sample requests from our plants, which are accustomed to handling bulk quantities with occasional 50-pound sample orders. We therefore arranged to send a supply of the material to a contract packager who repacked it into five-pound sample quantities and mailed sample packages out at our request.

Along with each sample went a letter describing the material, a post card enabling prospects to acknowledge receipt, and an evaluation form the user could fill out to describe his experience during evaluation. These later were valuable in eliminating unnecessary calls on the part of our already busy salesmen.

Of course, a lot of auxiliary forms printing was required to mechanize the sample-handling and inquiry-handling systems, but this was completed in time, thanks to the planning.

Once the planning was complete, and the various parts of the project in preparation, the chart helped to provide a control. As steps were completed, the blocks were filled in with a red pencil. Thus, the chart served as a visual control board.

The results of this program, undertaken and completed within less than two months, was an unqualified success. Six months after introduction we had received more than 4,000 inquiries. All were handled, screened, and either relegated to the "dead file" or turned over to our salesmen within six weeks after receipt.

And while sales figures are confidential, the curve, one year later, was rising exponentially. We were already past the "introduction" phase of a new-product introduction and well into the "growth" phase.

While the program put a greatly increased burden on both our salesmen and our technical people, neither group was at any time strained to the point where they had to pass up good prospects.

PERT, of course, is not the only timetable technique that can be used on new-product introductions. Other timetabling techniques can be equally satisfactory, especially if fewer communications techniques are utilized in the introduction. No matter how simple the introduction, however, some type of formal planning should be used to take into account the various lead times and the multiple steps needed to bring the program together in a reasonable time and in proper sequence so as to get maximum benefit from the dollars invested in communications.

BETWEEN RESPONSE AND SALE

Many marketers consider the job of mass communications complete at the point where an inquiry is received. From then on, they feel that the responsibility for follow-up falls to the sales department and that individual contact is the only technique that can be used for follow-up. In certain situations this may be true. Where the market is narrow, however, and where there is adequate sales manpower to handle the inquiries generated, direct sales follow-up probably represents the fastest and most effective road to success.

But most new-product-introduction situations do not meet these criteria. In most cases, this attitude represents not only a failure to use available marketing techniques, but it places an impossible burden on the sales force.

Typically, a significant new product introduced into a medium-size market will bring in between 3,000 and 10,000 inquiries. Many are from literature collectors, and many are from people who would like to use the product but may be unable to for reasons they cannot know from the initial information made available to them. Some, of course, are from potential buyers.

In the usual situation, only a limited number of salesmen are available. Because selling a new product usually involves a far greater number of steps than selling a mature product, the salesmen cannot handle as many customers and therefore are often completely tied up in pursuing a relatively small number of leads. If the job of following up the mountains of inquiries, many of which do not represent genuine potential buyers, is left to the salesmen, it will become so burdensome that inquiries beyond the first few simply will not get handled. And there will undoubtedly be real prospects among the ones that are missed.

If we look critically at the steps involved in following up inquiries, we find that those that occur up to the point of determining whether or not the inquirer is a true prospect are routine. Often those involved in taking the inquirer through the first few steps toward a sale are also routine. Once we determine what those steps are, they can be made routine as a matter of practice and put into the hands of people less qualified than the salesmen, thus leaving the latter with more free time to concentrate their efforts on the steps that must be individualized.

By setting up a detailed, step-by-step inquiry follow-up procedure, whose objective is to qualify the initial inquirers and to presell the prospective buyers, mass-communications techniques can greatly increase the efficiency of the marketing process. In a very real sense, such inquiry-handling procedures are similar to the procedures involved in a multipart direct-mail program. The only real difference is that in a direct-mail program, the wishes of the mailer determine the timing for each segment of the mailing program and all the mailers are sent out together. In an inquiry-handling procedure, the timing for sending out the segments of the program is determined by the action of the inquirer. Thus, while the planning and development work is similar, an inquiry-handling procedure requires more management of the mailing operation than does direct mail.

The steps involved in handling inquiries are usually very much the same, even for different types of products. Once an inquiry comes in, the usual response item is a piece of literature designed to provide the detailed information the inquirer may not have received from his initial communications exposure to the product. If the literature is properly prepared, and if it includes the detailed information that will enable the prospect to evaluate his potential use of the product, the inquirer will be in a position to know whether or not he is still interested in the product. But he may or may not be ready to communicate that interest to the company. So the next objective for mass communications is to solicit a response from him that clearly indicates his degree of interest. This can be done by direct-mail techniques if we are to be satisfied with a partial response, or by telephone follow-up if we want complete response. Often, enough qualification information can be developed at this stage to categorize the respondents according to probable potential. Or their particular sales resistance might be measured by these techniques, to be followed up with a mailing directed primarily at breaking down that resistance. Such follow-up information can be in the form of literature specifically prepared for the applications in which the inquirer is interested, or it might be standardized letters, a different letter for each type of response. Or it might be a computer-generated letter with specific paragraphs selected for particular situations.

The details of the technique will vary with the product and the market. And it must take into account the total number of people from whom inquiries are expected, as well as the number of salesmen available. The objective of the screening technique, of course, must be to reduce the number of in-person presentations to the number that the salesmen can physically handle. The criteria for segregating the screened inquiries must therefore be established with this goal in mind.

In a typical situation, where a large number of inquiries are solicited, the inquiry-handling follow-up procedure usually follows a pattern similar to the one diagramed in Figure 9. In this procedure, a piece of literature is sent out to each inquirer. Enclosed is a response card that asks for certain screening information, such as size of company, volume of potential use, degree of interest, and so on. During the two to three weeks following this step, one of two things can happen. Either the response card is returned or it is not. Usually, between 5 percent and 20 percent of such cards are returned.

Responses can be put into one of several categories: excel-

Figure 9. Typical inquiry-handling program.

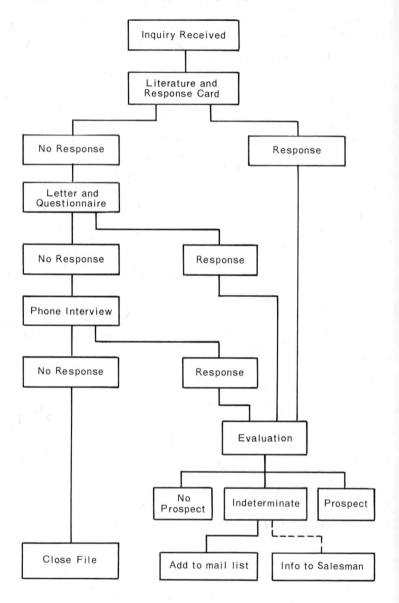

lent, poor, or indeterminate, with the preset screening criteria decisive. Each type must be handled differently, again according to a preset pattern. To those who failed to respond at this stage, a follow-up questionnaire is sent. This can be expected to achieve a 15 to 30 percent response level. These responses can then be classified in exactly the same way as the first response. For those who still haven't responded, a personal telephone call may be the answer, with either your employees or an outside service making the call and asking the qualifying questions. Since the person making the telephone calls will be operating from an established questionnaire, he or she will not have to be as well-trained or as highly paid as the already busy salesmen. Thus, for a cost considerably lower than that involved in salesman follow-up, some response is received from virtually all inquirers.

The step following classification varies from project to project. The best prospects are commonly turned over to the salesmen for personal follow-up. Those in the secondary classifications may be followed up on with additional literature, or with additional questions, or with a letter giving them a second opportunity to indicate their degree of interest. If the nature of the product and the screening mechanism is such that the inquirer will state his problem clearly in one of the screening-response steps, standardized answers to particular questions might be prepared and forwarded with a second screening follow-up.

The details of the procedure must, of course, be customized for each new-product situation. These steps take a lot of planning, and the administration of the program takes time and careful attention to detail. But the planning work need be done only once, and the administration can be accomplished by lower-cost and more readily available personnel than those involved in direct sales work. Thus a proper balance of replicated inquiry-handling procedures and sales follow-up, with the sales follow-up limited to only the most promising prospects, can give far better sales results per dollar than a system that relies solely on salesmen to do the inquiry follow-up.

Where a product has a relatively low unit price, and a sampling step is needed before people can qualify as real prospects, similar replicated communications techniques can be used throughout the sampling procedure and even through reporting on the evaluation of the samples. This permits the salesmen to spend their time on prospects who have already learned about the product, tested it, and indicated that it has promise in their operations.

The use of mass-communications techniques through the sampling steps is more applicable where the product is a relatively low-priced material or component than where it has a high unit value. The reason is that without in-person screening by salesmen, the likelihood of wasted samples is considerably higher. The additional cost of sampling at the earlier stage must be balanced against the higher productivity that results when the salesmen limit their time to people who have already passed a critical point in the buying process.

Where the material is relatively low-priced and needs evaluation, the extra time, energy, and money involved in planning and administering an inquiry-handling follow-up and sampling procedure can pay large dividends, save the salesmen time, shorten the cycle from inquiry to final sale, and move a product from introduction to full commercialization in a much shorter time than the usual techniques, which rely on salesmen handling the inquiry follow-up procedures.

One of the key guides to the acceptance of the new product is the information fed back from the field. Salesmen who can talk to prospects and learn at an early stage about product effectiveness, and who can uncover sales resistances that may have been unanticipated, or at least underrated, during the planning phase, provide the best source of this type of feedback. Assuming that the deficiencies and problems that are uncovered are relatively minor and are correctable, the product-introduction strategy and tactics, and even the product itself, may have to be adjusted to some degree in response to the new information. Thus the earlier the information is received, the faster the necessary modifications can be made to meet market needs.

One problem in relying on salesmen for the necessary feedback is that while the feedback can be thorough for each prospect covered, the number of people the salesmen contact is small enough that it is difficult to get a true perspective on the entire market. Here again, the mass-communications techniques can be used to develop this broader information. Once a potential problem is identified, a questionnaire that probes the problem more deeply can be sent to a sampling of an inquirer list or mailing list. Or the inquiry follow-up-procedure materials can be so adjusted as to make it possible to gather the information during the screening process. Thus the scope of the problem can be determined—if not more quickly than by direct feedback, at least more reliably, so that management can take action with greater assurance that it is moving in the right direction.

Similar research techniques can be used to follow up on prospects who have not taken action—in order to uncover some of the underlying reasons. A mail or telephone questionnaire by a third party can often uncover information that the prospective buyers are unwilling to provide directly to the salesmen.

In those areas where both salesmen and mass communications can do something of the same job, it is difficult to draw guidelines for the most efficient kind of program and to decide beforehand where the responsibility of one ends and the other begins. The cues for the optimum program usually come from the salesmen. Those with responsibility for mass communications should stay close to the activities of the salesmen, keeping in mind the primary objective of sparing salesmen time during the new-product-introduction phase. The mass-communications people should watch carefully for any activities that the salesmen have to repeat over and over. These are the activities where there is most likely to be economic justification for a mass-communications approach, one that will either relieve the salesman altogether of an onerous burden or reduce the time he must devote to it.

7

Administering
the New Product
Introduction

The basic management goals during the introductory phase are to insure the viability of the product and to achieve maximum market penetration in the shortest possible time. The goals during the latter stages of the growth and maturity phases are to optimize short- and long-term profits. While it is true that certain profit-optimization goals may exist during the introduction phase, they are usually secondary to, and in conflict with, the other more fundamental introductory objectives. If too much emphasis is placed on profitability during the introduction phase, as frequently occurs in industry, it has the effect of forcing the product into maturity too soon. Not only can this seriously endanger the viability of the product, but it can often limit the potential sales and profitability of the product for the remainder of its life cycle.

A key problem in new-product introduction is that almost never can one predict how long the introductory phase will last, or what problems will be encountered, or whether success will be achieved at all.

The project manager must make each of his decisions with prime consideration for the effect it will have on product success, secondarily on the effect it will have on the speed of market penetration, and only then on the effect it will have on current profits. Where the manager of a mature or maturing product must be largely concerned with setting firm, long-standing policies that will enable his organization to function effectively at minimum cost, the new-product manager must be ready to adjust policies as feedback indicates the need to do so. Above all, he must evaluate his expenditure alternatives in terms of the chances of success or failure, instead of short-term return on investment.

The management techniques of the new-product manager must be oriented toward condensing time rather than optimizing the profits. To maintain objectivity and fiscal responsibility, he must establish some sort of a dollar-value guideline for time. For example, he must keep in mind that at some date in the future he will be faced with a "go" or "no-go" decision. If the project is "go" after that time, his goal will switch to profit optimization. If it is "no-go," the plant, the salesmen, the support teams and the whole marketing operation will be shut down. What is it worth, then, if the no-go decision date is moved forward a month? Obviously, it is worth the total investment of time and out-of-pocket dollars by everyone involved in the new project for a one-month period. That analysis provides one figure for the value of time.

If, on the other hand, the introduction is successful and the philosophy converted to one suitable for a maturing product, the decision parameters for time value become far more complex. They will be related to the position in the market achieved at that point in time, as compared to the position achievable without taking the action under consideration. Since the profitability during the entire life cycle of the product is related to the share of market achieved when competition matches the product, the economic value of time depends largely on how close effective competition is. If it appears that competition is imminent, the value of time can be very high. If competitive reaction is still far off, and the company has the field to itself, then time is considerably less important.

Because the parameters for assigning proper value to time depend on the final outcome, it is far easier to make such a judgment after the project is complete. But the realities of business life force us to make such decisions at a time when we are surrounded by uncertainty. The money value of time falls somewhere between the continuing cost rate and the expected rate of profit attainable in the foreseeable future. Just where it falls is a matter of judgment. Despite the uncertainties in determining the value of shortening the time to the point of the go or no-go decision, the project manager should assign some realistic value to it as a basis for his investment and expense decisions.

Since time is the most important of the resources to be managed, most new-product management techniques should be directed toward getting the most from it. Timetable techniques should be utilized to the fullest, whether they are simply marked-up calendars or computerized PERT networks.

Because of the uncertainties in the exact timing of such areas as setting up customer meetings, making technical changes, and doing all the new things that have to be done in a new-product venture, and because of the many things that must reach completion together for maximum efficiency, the PERT program technique is probably the most effective for total venture management. In the previous chapter, we discussed a PERT program that was oriented toward the mass-communications and inquiry-follow-up segments of the introduction program. It takes little imagination to see how this same program can be expanded to include the tooling, production, technical, and sales steps that go along with the communications aspects in a new-product introduction.

Despite the time pressures that make planning an easy step to bypass, the project manager will save a great deal of time by planning and administering a detailed timetable. Because of the continually changing situation characteristic of the new-product introductory phase, timetables cannot be rigid. They must frequently be rearranged and replanned. If the project manager feels he does not have the time to do this planning, it should then become one of the key job functions that he delegates to his assistant—or even to his secretary, if she has the competence.

If PERT-type planning is not used, a periodic review of time goals should be made with every department involved in the product introduction. Each department's goal must, of course, fit within the overall time goals agreed on. It is obvious to anyone in the dynamic situation created by a new-product introduction that if either manufacturing or marketing outdistances the other by a significant margin, more time and money must have been utilized in that department than was necessary, while the project, as a whole, gains nothing from the extra activity. And if marketing is waiting for an equipment or material modification that it has found necessary, the technical people must maintain their timetables or the entire effort will mark time. Only if the timetables are administered together can the whole project be kept on course.

Beyond timing, the most difficult challenge to the new

product is to maintain production capability at a level sufficient to support sales, without overexpanding to the point
where costs are far out of line. Because lead time is normally
needed by manufacturing, capabilities must be based on sales
projections made one month, six months, or even two years in
advance. But sales projections for new products during the
introduction phase are rarely close to the mark. For long-lead
products, the problem of balancing production with sales can
be critical, and there is no single or easy solution. Sales
projections must simply be made as realistically as possible,
and accompanied by estimates of the maximum and minimum
demand at a number of future points in time. Manufacturing
goals should normally run somewhat above the probable sales
level, but whether or not it should be moved to the maximum
possible demand level depends very much on the investment
required and the efficiencies of scale involved in this particular product area.

UNEXPECTED PROBLEMS

No new-product introduction ever goes as planned. That
is a luxury reserved only for mature and declining products,
and even those generate their share of surprises. In new-
product introduction, the surprises are more frequent, simply
because there are more unknowns to deal with—more
unknowns in production, in market acceptance, in product
requirements, in cost of manufacturing, selling and servicing,
in market requirements, and even in management's patience
in supporting the introduction. The problems that arise
normally fall into four broad categories: product, production,
marketing, and financial control.

Product problems normally arise when initial contact

with the market indicates that the product has a deficiency that makes it partially or completely unacceptable to all or part of the market. Such deficiencies can often be corrected by re-engineering the product, or in the case of a material, by changing some of its properties. Sometimes this can be done quite easily, sometimes it is extremely difficult. Sometimes the change makes no significant difference in the cost of the product, but more often it raises costs significantly. When such problems arise and are identified, alternative solutions must be looked at in terms of the cost of making the change, as related to the need. If the product deficiency is so significant that it absolutely precludes selling in the market without a change, the choice becomes quite simple. Either make the change, or terminate the project. In most cases, however, such clear-cut problems are identified before the decision is made to go ahead. Consequently, problems that arise after introduction are usually less significant ones, whose greatest effect is on the depth of penetration that can be achieved and the speed with which sales can be made, rather than on whether or not the product will move at all.

Production problems are much more difficult to evaluate. Perhaps the prototype product that was market-tested before the introduction decision was made cannot be duplicated in the plant. Or quality-control problems lead to a large number of failures. Or the plant simply cannot produce at the design level, perhaps because of an earlier misassessment, or because vital equipment took longer to deliver than was expected, or because raw materials or components suppliers failed to live up to their promises. These problems, too, must be handled on an individual basis. And the cost of solving them must be balanced against the cost in time or the threat to the viability of the new product.

Marketing problems are equally difficult to assess. Unexpected market resistance can arise from a large number of directions. Perhaps the industry is slow in recognizing the problem that the new product has been designed to solve. Or it may have found a totally different solution. Or the delays in getting internal approval in buyer companies, and the delays in prospects' working their way through the evaluation and purchasing steps, may be greater than anticipated. Or experience may reveal that it takes more sales calls to complete a sale than was originally anticipated, with the result that the sales staff is far too small to cover the market. Or we may have failed in the initial planning steps to recognize an emotional or psychological hurdle that the product must surmount. A host of such marketing problems can arise, and when they do, they must be looked at critically and objectively so that an analysis can be made—not an easy thing to do where information is subjective and the analyzers may be emotionally involved. Once the analysis is made, and the scope of the problem is defined, alternative courses of action must be costed out. The modified marketing strategy and tactics that result from this analysis must then be reevaluated in light of the severity of the problem. It will almost always require additional funds to solve midstream problems, so these costs must be evaluated against the standards of product viability and the value of time outlined above.

Financial problems can also arise in midstream, and they may arise from several sources. If the new product relied on venture capital for its initial financing, the venture capital was probably not made available in a lump sum. The usual pattern is for initial capital to be made available with the promise of future capital as the need arises. If an external factor such as a stock market decline, or other loss of capital resources by the financing group, or even a change of heart, occurs, the secondary financing needed as the program progresses might simply not be made available. The problem can be remarkably similar in a segment of a large company, despite the broader based financial resources of such an organization. Where the company may have made a commitment to support the product during its introductory phase, a change in profitability in other areas that takes place during the development and introduction period of the new product may make the corporation unable or unwilling to provide it with the continuing support it needs. It frequently happens that a major corporation, when faced with broad profitability problems, slashes away in a wholesale manner at the unprofitable segments of its business. That many of these are new-product areas that are still in their introduction phase does not seem to warrant special consideration. A surprising number of new products are aborted every year for just this reason.

The solution to midstream financing problems in either the small-company or big-company environment is not easy to find. The obvious solution, to resell the initial financing source or go after other sources of money, can drain so much manpower from the important functions of managing and marketing the new product that this in itself will cripple the product. And once one sponsor has lost interest in the product, it is extremely difficult to sell a second.

The solution probably lies in facing up to the problem of changes in financial support level at an early stage. Normally the fact that financial support is drying up is known well in advance of the time when funds run out. But the thought is so devastating that the manager of the new product refuses to face the prospect and goes along with business as usual in the hope that his guardian angel will appear before the well runs dry. And too often it simply does not happen.

As soon as the danger of insufficient funding arises, the

project manager should reevaluate his goals, and his new goals must be very short-range ones. The long-range maximum market-penetration goal may be replaced by one aimed at having the project salable at the point when the funds run dry. This normally involves draining funds from the longer-range type of projects and putting them into whatever area of new-product introduction is running the slowest. Usually that segment is marketing. Thus where a product-introduction strategy might originally have been aimed at attacking the market on a broad front, the impending shortage of funds may require that all but the most promising segment of the market be temporarily ignored. Then, by the time funds run out, the new project may have had sufficient success in the narrow market to be able to stand on its own feet on a much smaller scale, and thus demonstrate the viability of the new product sufficiently to attract capital from other sources, or to convince a corporate management group that the product warrants continued support.

WHEN TO ABORT THE PRODUCT

One of the most difficult questions in managing a new product arises when the product is running into difficulties. The question is whether or not it should be aborted. A large number of products, perhaps as many as 80 percent, simply do not make it. Probably at least 50 percent are doomed to failure from the beginning. The reason may be in the product, or as frequently happens, the market conditions may have changed during the course of development and introduction so that the new product no longer fulfills the market need for which it was designed. Or it may be that the production staff was grossly in error in estimating the cost of producing the item. But whatever the reason, a time arises when there is a clear-cut need for a go or no-go decision on whether or not to continue the new product.

In the consumer package-goods area a large body of information exists relating recognition ratings and repurchase rates with expected rates of sales growth, which, when handled by operations research-type analysis, can provide reasonable guidance as to whether or not the product will be viable. In the industrial market, with its larger number of variables, it is unlikely that enough historic information can ever be developed to make such an analytical approach possible. Instead, we must rely on the judgments of the people involved. It is reasonable, of course, to assume that if the product has been on the market for a period of time, and the sales volume fails to grow and therefore remains below the breakeven point, the product is doomed to failure. But such clear-cut situations are rare. In the more common situation there is discernible growth, but the question is whether or not the growth is sufficient to carry the product to profitability levels in time to justify its investment.

No attempt can be made from this vantage point to analyze the many factors involved, or even to guide the reader to the proper type of analysis. The factors that go into the analysis vary too greatly from product to product, market to market, and even from company accounting system to company accounting system. But one thing should be clear to the project manager—the question of whether or not the product is viable and should be continued will arise at at least one point in the product-introduction cycle. To continue the project beyond such a point, if it has no hope, can be a costly error. To kill it when it is at the point where a little more time could carry the product over the brink to success can be an even more costly error.

One of the things that the project manager should keep in mind throughout the introduction segment of the cycle is that when that question arises, he will be far more likely to make the proper decision if he has as many answers as possible. Nothing will delay the decision more than a lack of input information upon which to base such a decision. Thus his product-introduction plan should provide for adequate support for all segments of the introduction. Though the cost may be high, it avoids the problem, at the point of decision, as to whether the product would not be successful if it were better supported by technical service, advertising, salesmen, and so on.

If inadequate support has been given too many areas, the project manager will find it very difficult to make the go or no-go decision on any basis but an extremely subjective one. But if all controllable areas have been given full support, the variables left for judgment will be few enough that the project manager will be more likely to evaluate this smaller number of unknowns correctly. In the face of a large number of unanswered questions, the usual course is to continue the project until the answers emerge, a course that usually costs far more than it would have cost to make an adequate investment in the first place.

An error commonly made is to provide far too little mass communications in the original plan. Six months later the choice will be between killing the project or giving it the necessary support. If the second decision is made, and it turns out the reason for failure lies in other areas, the cost to the company is far greater than it would have been had adequate support been provided at the beginning.

As a general rule, if an early-stage expenditure can move the go or no-go decision forward by a month at a cost lower than a month's overhead, it is a good investment to make.

TRANSITION TO THE GROWTH PHASE

The product-introduction phase has a relatively clear-cut beginning—the point in time where the decision to introduce is made. Its end point, however—the point where the introduction phase ends and where the growth phase begins—is far more difficult to define, even from the vantage point of later history. And during the period of time involved when that transition takes place it is almost impossible to define.

In principle, the product-introduction phase can be thought of as ending at that point in time when the sales organization and sales policies are reasonably stable and when there is no longer a serious question about the viability of the product. In a large company this can occur at a clear-cut point in time when responsibilities are taken out of the hands of the task force that had responsibility for developing, manufacturing, and marketing the product, and given to the people who normally have responsibility for those functions. At this point, management philosophies and techniques consistent with mature and maturing product needs supplant the entrepreneurial approaches needed for successful development and introduction.

The beginning of the growth phase of the product life cycle, as differentiated from the introduction phase, occurs when the product can stand on its own feet economically and produce a profit without sacrificing its growth potential to accomplish this. From this point in time, decisions must be evaluated against short- and long-range profit optimization, rather than on the basis of proving the viability of the project.

The transition from the goal of rapid market penetration to that of short-term profits is a key characteristic of the growth phase of the life cycle of the product. Thus the beginning of the growth phase is the point where short-term profit goals begin to be considered. Thus at this point there must still be some concern with the speed at which market penetration can be achieved, though that will of course diminish as further market penetration is achieved and saturation is approached.

Beyond changes in attitude and objectives, the transition from the introduction phase to the growth phase calls for changes in organization structure. Where the organization structure during the product-introduction phase had to be kept somewhat loose to adapt to changing requirements, and where interfaces between people with different responsibilities had to be flexible, the organizational structure during growth and maturity must be clearly drawn, with responsibilities clearly assigned. With the objective changing to profit optimization, each department must look carefully to minimizing its operating costs and substituting efficiency for mere effectiveness as its prime operating goal.

The project manager must be aware that these changes have to be made, and must lead the way in making them before the financial reports point out their need. For the freewheeling, fast-moving type of organization that operates most effectively in the new-product-introduction environment can destroy all profitability for a product if allowed to continue to so operate during the growth phase, when profitability becomes the primary objective.

Where a big company is so structured that the product is in the hands of one group during the introductory phase and is later integrated into the company's normal operating pattern, the problem of conversion to the growth phase is totally different. If the regular manufacturing department is to take over manufacture of the new product, and the regular sales department is to take over its sales, then the transition of responsibilities must be planned in every bit as much detail as the initial introduction of the product itself. Those people who have been involved in the new product during its introductory phase should be given temporary assignments within the departments that are taking over product responsibility, at least until people with new responsibility have a thorough education and some experience in the new-product area. As an alternative, people from the established departments can be assigned to the new-product group before the transition is made. Whether the training period needed is two months or two years depends largely on the nature of the product and the characteristics of the market.

Because of the difficulties in making the transition from one group to another, and the possible danger of retarding the product's progress during the transition period, people from the team that has been involved with the new product during its introduction phase frequently become associated with it permanently. This course has the advantage of assuring continuity of product management, though with it comes the disadvantage that the experience gained in the techniques of introduction of the new product are probably lost to the next new product to come along.

THE MANAGEMENT INTERFACE

It would be easy to close this volume on the note that "what is good for the new product is good for the company" and that everybody involved in the various decisions to be made will be equally objective and knowledgeable. But that would not be facing the facts of corporate life—that the problems of new-product introduction are not only the problems of properly dealing with the market but the internal problems of dealing with a corporate management as well.

Normally, when a new product appears at the outset to be highly significant to a company, the corporate management will become heavily involved in all the decisions relating to product development and introduction. Whether this is a new company formed to develop and market the product, or a small company that is making a major investment in the new product, or a large company that is making an investment in the new product that represents a relatively high percentage of its capital, there is no problem of a new-product–management interface. In all these cases, the true management of the new product is the management of the corporation.

But in the more common situation, where the new product in its earlier stages represents only a small portion of the investment of the company, the new-product decisions are made largely by people operating at a functional level considerably below that of corporate management. Here, very serious problems can exist that arise from a variety of factors. The most important one is that management, being somewhat separated from the details of the new-product development, tends to evaluate the new product by the same criterion it uses for the more established operations—the key criterion of short-term profitability.

Because of this orientation, management is often in too much of a hurry to derive profits from the new venture. The result is that it withholds additional funds that are often needed, and the new product is forced to produce revenue before it has proved its viability in the market and before it has established sufficient penetration to assure its future. This forces the new-product group to make decisions that will inevitably hurt the product, or at a minimum, will keep it from achieving its true potential.

Management of an established company often fails, too, to

recognize the differing needs of new products serving a market different from the one the company has been exposed to in the past. The ratios of sales expense to dollar sales, for example, or advertising per dollar of sales, or inventory turnover, or credit policies needed to satisfy the new market, may be vastly different from those in the fields in which the company has experience. Management may therefore fail to approve the budget and policy decisions that would be in the best interests of the product, and force such decisions to be consistent with those for the other, unrelated segments of the company. The net result may be an unnecessary product failure.

Another problem arises when management changes its goals. Too often, financial trouble in one segment of the company will force economies throughout the entire company, including that segment of the company that is trying to establish its new-product entry. Where other segments of the company may be slightly hurt by the changed management demand for greater short-term profits, the new product may be damaged irreparably. Even if it survives, it may be forced to settle for an earlier maturity and a smaller share of the business than it deserves.

Still another problem can arise when the product involves a technology that is unfamiliar to management. Unable to evaluate the product's merits and the product's investment needs on the basis of first-hand understanding, management is forced to evaluate the project on the basis of its faith in the judgments of the people who have such knowledge. Because these people are frequently too many steps below the level of decision-making, management tends to put less faith in their judgment. But the people management trusts, who are normally higher on the corporate ladder, may not have the needed depth of understanding in the new technology. Thus a communications gap can develop that often makes it impossible for the true costs, the true risks, and the true potential payoff to be communicated to management in a way that gives it faith in either the facts or the conclusions.

The fact that new-product introductions rarely go as planned, and that new products frequently take more time to reach profitability levels than initial projections promise, has the effect of continually lowering the credibility of the project group in the minds of corporate management. As this credibility declines, so does the willingness of management to invest further. The net result is that many projects are denied financial support at just the point where such support can have the greatest payoff.

The new project manager must always keep these potential problems in mind. Rather than direct all his energies to ensuring the direct success of the project, he must devote some of them to maintaining not only close communication but also his credibility with top management. He should take pains to keep at least one person who operates within top management circles completely aware of the needs, policies, potential markets, and, to the greatest extent possible, the technology of the new product. This individual can then serve as spokesman in the management discussions that will decide the fate of the project.

In almost any new-project introduction, greater demands will be made than management originally expects, so the project manager had best develop an internal strategy and support it with the necessary tactics to make sure that his product will survive not only the ravages of the marketplace, but the uncertainties of an increasingly distrustful management group.